Don Williams'

Inside the ADIRONDACK BLUE LINE

Don Williams'

Inside the
ADIRONDACK
BLUE LINE

Don Williams

Illustrated by John Mahaffy

NORTH COUNTRY BOOKS
Utica, New York

Don Williams'
INSIDE THE ADIRONDACK BLUE LINE

by
Don Williams

Copyright © 1999

ISBN 0-925168-65-3

Published by
North Country Books, Inc.
311 Turner Street
Utica, New York 13501

*Dedicated to all those who shared
their Adirondack memories,
both written and oral,
that our humble writings might
reach a new generation of those
called Adirondackers.*

Contents

Preface

New York's Adirondack Mountain country may be the most written about region in the United States. Publications have flowed like an Adirondack stream since the early 1850's when *The Hunting Excursion to Louis Lake* was penned and Jebediah Huntington wrote the first Adirondack novel, *The Forest*. S. H. Hammond and Joel Headley soon followed with their Adirondack stories. Adirondack Murray began his Adirondack tales and Irving Bacheller's bestseller, *Eben Holden*, hit the bookstores. And so it went. There appears to be an endless supply of written and oral history on the Adirondacks.

The Adirondack "blueline" was drawn on the maps in 1890 to encircle the six million-acre Adirondack State Park—a mixture of public and private lands. The stories of those who spent their lives inside the "blueline" and of those who visited inside the "blueline" provide a memorable and unique picture of mankind's relation to New York's forested mountains. The natural attributes of the region provide another aspect worthy of attention.

The citizens of New York added "forever wild" protection to the Adirondacks in the 1894 New York State Constitution. Thus, the Adirondack state-owned lands are preserved for us today.

The one hundred Adirondack stories printed here preserve a portion of the oral and written history of life in the Adirondacks. Take a trip "Inside the Adirondack Blue Line" and meet the early settlers, visitors, guides, writers, artists, and others. Delve into geology and geography, flora and fauna. Renew your own Adirondack memories and create some new ones. And remember, the Adirondacks are still there waiting for you to add your own Adirondack story.

—*DRW*

I

Adirondack Country

INSIDE THE ADIRONDACK BLUELINE

The Adirondack "BLUELINE" may be a mystery to the uninformed but to an Adirondacker it is as important to our history as the Mason-Dixon Line. The hundred-year-old line forms a political and somewhat geographic boundary around the best piece of real estate in America, the Adirondack Park. Those inside the Blueline live under zoning regulations special to the region. The Park contains twelve counties (Hamilton and Essex entirely within the Line), eighty-five towns, and fourteen villages.

The "blue"line came about in 1890, possibly because the Forest Commissioners did not have a green pencil the day they drew a line on the map which encompassed the land for the, then-proposed, Adirondack Park.

Parks had come into their own in our nation during the middle of the century and the Adirondack Park was part of a need felt by New York's citizens. People had been going to local cemeteries to enjoy the out-of-doors and the idea of an outdoor park gained popularity. Many humans function better when they can escape urbanization.

The Park had its promoters. Verplanck Colvin, one of the Adirondack greats, spent twenty-eight years surveying the Adirondacks and promoting the idea of the Park. Speaking at Lake Pleasant in 1868, he proposed the creation of an Adirondack state park or forest preserve. He urged public action to stop any further desecration of the forests. He followed up in 1870 with a report to the Legislature on preserving the Adirondacks primarily as a watershed.

The Legislature played its role, establishing a commission in 1872 to study saving Adirondack lands for a public park. By 1885 they were ready to pass a law establishing the Forest Preserve and in 1892 they established the Adirondack Park by passing further legislation. In 1894 the State Constitution protected the Adirondack Forest Preserve as "forever wild."

The Forest Commission submitted a report to the Legislature on April 28, 1891, covering their 1890 annual report. A section was devoted to the discussion of a proposed Adirondack Park and a land map with a "blue line" indicating the proposed boundaries was submitted.

Thus, the Adirondack BLUELINE is over one hundred years old.

Today's Adirondack Park contains six million acres with almost half owned by the people of New York State. This was not always true. New York took possession of some seven million acres north of the Mohawk River after the Revolution. By 1885 they had sold off and given away all but 700,000 acres. After the creation of the Preserve, New York began the process of buying and retaking the former state-owned lands. Lucky for us our forefathers had the foresight, for whatever reason, to save some land for our use and the use of future generations. The once-expected large metropolitan areas and vast railroad systems never materialized in the harsh Adirondack wilds and we have the great wilderness to enjoy.

Some say the Adirondacks is unusual. Larger than the combined areas of Yellowstone, Yosemite, Grand Canyon, Glacier, and Olympic national parks; it is a mixture of public and private lands. Some lands are tracts of unbroken state wilderness and others are a checkerboard of public and private holdings. Regulated by the Land Use and Zoning Regulations, the State Land Master Plan governs the use of the State-owned lands.

The Preserve lands are classified in nine basic categories: wilderness, primitive, canoe, wild forest, intensive use, historic, state administrative, wild, scenic and recreational rivers, and travel corridors. Each classification has its own definition and use.

Private lands within the Blueline are governed by the Private Land Use and Development Plan. The six categories include hamlet, moderate intensity use, low intensity use, rural use, resource management, and industrial use. These categories determine what the owners can do with their lands.

New Yorkers can be proud of their Blueline. They have done what no others have done; the citizens of New York have preserved a great wilderness area for generations to come. And as each year passes on this earth it becomes more important to the very survival of the world's people.

MAPPING THE ADIRONDACKS

Sometimes it appears that there is an endless supply of maps of the Adirondack region of New York State. Modern mapmakers attempt to fill the needs of hikers, homeowners, tourists, sportsmen and others who want to find their way in the Adirondacks. The old-time mapmakers made do with the information that was available at the time.

A 1757 map developed for the French and Indian Wars labeled the Adirondacks, "Parts but little known?" Governor Pownal's map of the northern British colonies of 1776 took care of the Adirondacks:

This Vast
Track of Land
Which is the Antient
Couchsachrage, one of the Four
Beaver Hunting Countries
of the Six Nations
is not yet
surveyed.

The Samuel Holland Map of 1776 reached the conclusion:

This Country is not only uninhabited
but even unknown.

The John Eddy 1818 map of New York State printed a "warning" on the Adirondack country:

A wild barren tract extends hereabouts,
the property of the State, covered with
almost impenetrable Bogs
Marshes and Ponds, and Uplands with
Rocks and Evergreens.

The old Adirondacker said that he never got lost. "I just face south and there is north right behind me!" he explained. Not so easy. Standing in the midst of the giant pines and maples of the Adirondacks, a mapless/compassless intruder would find it difficult to differentiate north from south. Maps have a long Adirondack history and tell the story of man's relationship to the great wilderness of New York State.

Early maps called the Adirondacks, "Couchsachrage Country," or beaver hunting ground of the Native Americans. Guy Johnson gave the land to them on his 1771 map by declaring: "The boundary of New York, not being closed this part of the country, shall belong to the Mohawks." In 1775 the British Colony Map simply noted, "by reason of mountain swamps and drowned lands, are impassable and uninhabited." The map in New York State Education Leaflet No. 7 by the state archeologist also shows the Adirondacks as "uninhabited." Most early maps depicted the Adirondacks as a vast empty spot in upstate New York. Detailed maps of the Adirondacks were unavailable to the early excursionists.

Man was moving into the Adirondacks. State-owned lands were being claimed by wilderness settlers. Loggers ignored the unmarked and unprovable boundaries. Speculators were purchasing lands from the early investors. Court cases multiplied to settle land disputes. Railroads were planning routes for their iron rails. Trails were turning into roads. Inaccurate maps were creating chaos in Adirondack land dealings and tax collections.

A savior appeared on the scene. Scientist, lawyer, author, lecturer, surveyor Verplanck Colvin saw the need for an accurate map of the Adirondack lands. He was appointed Superintendent of the Adirondack Survey in 1882 and his twenty-eight-year Adirondack career began. He turned his genius mind to developing methods of obtaining an accurate survey and his robust body to enduring the conditions in the Adirondack wilderness of the last century. His relentless work, unsurpassed by any other, reflects the dedication and expertise he brought to the task.

Colvin grew up in a wealthy, well-known Albany family and received the best of education. He practiced law, taught at Hamilton College, lectured at the Albany Institute, and developed a deep interest in surveying and the Adirondacks. He discovered map errors caused by using compass needle measurements during his years in dealing with land transactions in court. Ore beds in the mountains caused the magnetic compass to give false readings. Therefore, he developed new methods of surveying to produce accurate maps.

A local newspaper of June 3, 1897 reported that Verplanck Colvin, Superintendent of State Land Surveys, and a corps of surveyors would start Monday moving from Little Falls to survey the boundary line between Herkimer and Hamilton counties. "Some property owners along the line have escaped taxation because the authorities did not know in which county the land was situated. It is claimed that several hotels on the Fulton Chain of Lakes do not pay taxes on this account." Thus, Colvin's survey would be used to establish ownership of Adirondack lands.

Colvin drove his guides and assistants relentlessly to complete the Adirondack survey and to produce accurate maps. His guides worked until their clothes were tattered and their shoes were worn through. He proposed the preserving of the Adirondacks. He predicted the need of

Adirondack waters by downstate communities. He produced yearly detailed reports not only on surveying, but on the plants and animals, and mountains and rivers, of the Adirondacks. His work stands out as unequalled in history.

Colvin, Adirondack mapmaker, ended his years a bitter man. Politics kept him from completing his work to his self-imposed high standards and his final report was not printed until this past year, a hundred years late.

Present day Adirondackers can make good use of topographical maps from the U. S. Geological Service but we are indebted to Verplanck for his pioneering work on the Adirondack survey. His maps defined the boundaries and the topo maps provide the details of the lands and waters on forty-five quadrangle maps of the Adirondack region. Getting lost is not so likely with today's maps, a good compass, and the work done by the impeccable Verplanck Colvin.

Today's Adirondackers rely on the Topographical Maps published by the United States Geological Survey. They each contain 153 bits of information useful to those who penetrated wilderness. They come in quadrangles and it takes some forty-five of them to cover the Adirondack region. Most sport shops and bookstores carry a supply.

Serious Adirondackers should consider the Adirondack Land Maps produced by the Department of Environmental Conservation. They are periodically updated and published in four sections. They contain a separation of the private and public lands and where they lie in relation to the original purchases. Other information includes an index to the Geological Survey Maps, easements, fire towers, and the usual geographic features.

Those who possess an old Esso Map of New York State have one of the best maps for locating Adirondack landmarks from the highways. The Esso Company was noted for placing the Adirondack mountain peaks on their maps. It made it possible to pick them out on a touring trip of the highways or to locate them for a hike. Too bad the day of free maps at the service stations had to end; they meant more to the general public than splashy TV ads.

Adirondack maps have evolved with the use of the Adirondacks. They have graduated from an empty wasteland spot on a New York State map to a detailed map to meet the needs of the many publics who use the mountains. In fact, the Adirondacks have reached the modern world with a map photographed from outer space.

ADIRONDACK LAND PURCHASES

Do you want to buy some choice Adirondack land for five cents an acre? Go back in time a century and a half or more and it becomes possible. The early purchases of the "vast wastelands" were models of graft, corruption, and influence, and highly underpriced. They involved wealthy investors, railroads, Native Americans, and politicians.

Alexander Macomb made the largest purchase of Adirondack lands. Two hundred years ago he purchased some four million acres in Lewis, Jefferson, Oswego, Herkimer, St. Lawrence, and Franklin Counties for eight pence per acre. Macomb had made a fortune in the fur trade and had married Philip Livingston's daughter. His influence was well-established and he had friends in high places. Governor George Clinton and Attorney General Aaron Burr were accused of taking a payoff to support the sale. Macomb's Purchase had a history of sales, resales, contracts unfulfilled, and mortgages foreclosed. Macomb received his first land patent in January 1792, and broke the land up into townships of 32,000 acres each. (Towns are political subdivisions and townships are geographic subdivisions).

About the same time Macomb started a new bank and became involved in some wrong-doing. He was in jail by April of 1792. The records indicate that he transferred his land interests in the Adirondacks to William Constable.

By 1798 Macomb was back on his feet, purchasing land on the highway going from Albany to New York City. He built a stone mansion and a grist mill. He failed again and ended up dying a poor man in 1831 at the home of Army Commander-in-Chief, Alexander Macomb, Jr. in Georgetown, D.C.

Apparently, Macomb had two wealthy friends associated with his great purchase of Adirondack lands. William Constable was a successful merchant who had trading ships bringing in goods from China. His son later built a mansion in Constableville which is now open to the public.

The other name which appears with Macomb in his purchases was Daniel McCormick. His fortune was made in banking. A bachelor, he was the last resident-owner of a home on Wall Street in New York City.

The actual relationship of the three investors is unknown. Macomb's first patent was for 1,920,000 acres. Six months after he bought it, he gave it to William Constable. Constable sold over a million acres to Samuel Ward the same year but the deal collapsed and he got it back. Macomb never received clear title to the three tracts he assigned to Daniel McCormick in 1795 and 1798. In spite of the transfers the First Commissioners Report of 1893 contains a copy of the final patent which was still called Macomb's Patent.

In most of the land deals the Native Americans were part of the agreement. Macomb reserved part of his purchase for the Indian Reservation at St. Regis, possibly in return for their approval of the sale.

The oldest of the great Adirondack land deals was called the Totten and Crossfield Purchase. The two were shipwrights doing business in New York City who lent their names to the purchase. This was common practice in business deals to disguise the identity of the real buyers.

The purchase should have been called the Jessup's Purchase. Edward and Ebenezer Jessup, friends of Sir William Johnson, English governors Dunmore and Tryon, were the buyers. To avoid the troublesome task of dealing with the Indians, the King of England declared that all transactions needed Crown approval. The Jessups needed the friendship of Johnson, Dunmore and Tryon to close the deal.

After the French and Indian War the Jessups began to develop some land in the Upper Hudson-Lake George region. They acquired land in Hamilton, Essex and Warren Counties. By 1770 they became the first Adirondack lumbermen, rafting logs on the Sacandaga, Schroon and Hudson. They built homes at Luzerne. The Revolution ended their activities in the Adirondacks; they were loyalists and left the country.

The original purchase by the Jessups was passed by the Native Americans in 1772 at Johnson Hall and included "800,000 acres" which in reality became 1,150,000 acres of Adirondack land. It cost them three pence an acre plus bribes.

The Totten and Crossfield Purchase was divided into fifty townships of 24,000 acres each which ran on a unique diagonal slant. (Check your Adirondack deed today and you will see it.) After the Revolution some townships were given to the original owners and some were sold by New York State. Dr. Benjamin Brandreth purchased a township for $3,000. In 1855 New York State sold three townships to a railroad for five cents an acre. Today, we, the people of New York State, own a large part of the purchase around Raquette Lake, Long Lake, Blue Mountain Lake, Indian Lake, Mt. Marcy, Indian Pass, the

Iron Works, and Jessups Lake and River.

Today's deeds contain references to the early Adirondack purchases but the days of buying huge tracts are gone forever. Good Adirondack land demands a high price and is in limited supply. It is impossible to do what one old Adirondacker explained, "I don't want to buy the whole Adirondacks, I just want to get that which borders on mine!"

II

Adirondack Boyhood

ADIRONDACK FARMBOY

Growing up in an Adirondack farmhouse was a memorable experience. Many speak fondly of the good 'ole days (and the good 'ole nights) and, in many ways, I guess they were. We each need to judge for ourselves those unforgettable experiences from our past that are so foreign to our lives today. Maybe I was the last of a long line of Adirondack farm boys but I would not trade it for anything.

Farming in the Adirondacks has always been a poor gamble at best; the rocky soils combined with the short growing season do not contribute to the growing of the giant pumpkins and corn the early settlers expected. The giant white pine and maples get acclimated to the weather much as the hardy, independent settlers who reside there.

Someone once said that they woke up on the Fourth of July and went on a summer picnic. The next day fall began. Short summers and harsh winters made life in the Adirondacks a challenging existence; money was scarce, labor saving devices were non-existent, and the work was hard.

Water, one of life's required sustainers, is plentiful in the Adirondacks but it was not always where you wanted it. Ours was at the bottom of a deep hole in the front yard. The old iron pump squeaked and groaned as we got our daily exercise by pumping up and down to lift the sweet well water to the old bucket. Our patience was always tried, especially on a cold, winter day, by the repeated shots of priming water needed to get the pump 'agoing.

The water was taken into the house in a bucket, summer and winter, and placed on the kitchen sink drain. The dipper hung by the pail and, when thirsty, we scooped out a drink and drank from the dipper. Families did not worry about family germs.

Saturday night was bath night for six children. It was an experience. A large tub was placed on the old kitchen stove and filled, bucket by bucket, with water. Hot water was dipped into a round galvanized tub in front of the stove. Luckily for me, my brothers did not like hot water so I got the first bath while the water was clean. A privacy sheet was hung up on a rope as we got older.

Studies have shown that a fish will only grow as large as the amount of water he is in. A bullhead in a ten gallon container will grow to ten inches and then stop. I was careful not to grow too large for that old galvanized tub. I grew a foot in my first year of college where they had larger bathtubs.

Washday was once a week and involved most of the family. Mom was the foreman and made the decisions. Water had to be carried and heated. In the early days the clothes were washed in a tub using a large plunger to move them up and down. Washboards took off the stubborn dirt. The old wooden ringer was turned by hand by one of the boys and the girls hung the clothes on the outside clothesline to dry. When we bought a new electric wringer washer, labor saving was brought to our Adirondack home.

Many winters the well went dry. Water had to be drawn in barrels on the sleigh from a pond behind the pasture about half-a-mile away. The cows had to be taken to the water every night after school. Did you ever take a frisky cow out of the barn in the middle of winter? Picture a bouncing, jumping cow racing through the snowy pasture land with two young boys holding on to the end of an inch-thick rope for dear life. We did not take the cow to water, she took us. Jasper Cropsy's serene painting, THE ADIRONDACKS, depicts a couple boys watering some passive cows at the base of an Adirondack mountain. It was not always as it was pictured.

Another never-forgotten winter activity was the trip to the outhouse, the privy. Discreetly located behind the garage it was a one hundred-yard walk or dash, depending on the weather, from the back door of the house. The old two-holer served us well. It never backed-up, broke down, or needed any replacement parts.

It was an unwritten rule that the boys stayed away from the little wooden house when the girls were using it. The poked-out knotholes helped with ventilation. Privacy was also ensured by the rope handle latched over a bent nail. The Sears and Roebuck catalog hung on a nail and the non-glossy pages were used up first.

Our house was heated by the big iron stove in the kitchen and a wood heater in the living room. The big kitchen table took the place of a dining room. Bedrooms were not heated except for what heat found its way up the stairway. The windows were covered by blankets and with flannel sheets and a couple dogs we kept warm. (You have heard of a two-dog night when the temperature drops below freezing.) We did most of our dressing and undressing around the living room stove.

We spent many hours listening to the radio, eating popcorn and ice cream, doing our homework, and just talking around that warm stove. Cutting and splitting the cords of wood needed to get us through the winter was another labor intensive job for the male members of the family. I always enjoyed seeing a full woodbox of wood by the stove.

Growing up in the Adirondacks differs from today's upbringing but the experience is worth remembering; it makes us a little more thankful for what we enjoy today.

SPEAKIN' ADIRONDACKISH

I have become a national authority on the Adirondack language. I speak Adirondackish. It is not a result of my lengthy college education but because I have spent my life listening to those who are true Adirondackers. They (we) have a language all their own.

I did not know that I spoke Adirondackish. At one point in my career I attended a national conference in New Jersey. During a discussion session (where much is said about nothin') a gentleman from one of the western states, who happened to be a scholar of dialects and languages, leaned across the table and said, "You are from the Adirondacks in upstate New York aren't you?"

I answered in surprise, "Why yes I am, but how did you know? "

"I recognized your dialect and the way that you pronounced certain words," he explained. It was then I first knew that I spoke Adirondackish. I had led a sheltered life in Northville and thought that everyone talked like I did.

My command of the Adirondack language has now become a matter of national record. It has reached a new level. Adirondack storyteller, John Vinton from New York City, once stayed at my Gloversville "great camp." He said that he learned to speak Adirondackish from listening to me and reading my writings. Much of what he learned he gained from reading my Oliver Whitman book. The phonetic spelling I used in the text made it easy for him to pick it up.

When Vinton's new book, "A Treasury of Great Adirondack Stories" was written for the Centennial of the Adirondack Park, he immortalized my contribution to Adirondackish. "The language style and some local details are derived from the journals of Oliver H. Whitman, a guide from Wells, as transcribed in Donald R. Williams, "Oliver H.

Whitman, Adirondack Guide (1979)" [now out-of-print], he wrote. Sometimes the pen is more powerful than intended; Oliver and I did not realize that we were providing a record of Adirondackish.

My early experiences with language was limited. When I was growing up some of the older folks told a story of the popular conductor on the F.J.and G. train from Gloversville to Sacandaga Park. When the train arrived at Cranberry Creek he would loudly announce, "Clanberry Cleek, Clanberry Cleek!"

I was always amused by this story until someone once asked me why I always said "Cranberry Crick" instead of "Cranberry Creek." I thought a small body of running water was a crick. In the Adirondacks a creek is a crick.

And so it is with many other words. A partridge is a "patridge" once it is inside the Blueline. The game protector is the "game proctor." Ginseng is "gingshang." There is no "g" on most "ing" words such as "runnin, eatin, or sleepin". Forest fires were a problem in the early Adirondacks. No one fought the fires, in the Adirondacks. You "fit the fire."

Many words are shortened in the Adirondacks, possibly because of the harsh outdoor environment. Probably becomes "probly," don't is "don," them is "em," next is "nex," until is "til" and going to is "gonna." "A" is left off of the "A" words. The lake is "bout a mile long" not about. You row "cross" the lake not across. "He got nother deer" not another. And a grouchy person is "cross and crabid!"

Some words take on new sounds. To is usually "ta"; "I'm goin ta school." "Unless" is rarely used. "Adirondackers never like to talk "lessen" they are alone or with someone". "For" becomes "fer".

Place names in the Adirondacks can be tricky. Adirondackers do not always agree on the pronunciation. I call Santanoni, "Sant-a-no-ni", while others say "San-ta-noni". The Abenaki Indians, who plied the Adirondacks, are called "Ab-not-keys" while the correct Adirondack pronunciation is "A-ben-a-keys". Outsiders have trouble with Piseco which is "pa-seek-o". "Vlaie" is prounced "fly". Adirondackish is not an easy language to learn.

Beyond the individual pronouncing of words, Adirondackers used their favorite expressions. Charlie Reese, longtime guide, introduced his Adirondack theories with "In my estimation, in my estimation". Another storyteller interspersed his narration with "frincetents" which I found out in later years was "for instance." And when Adironackers are saying "goodbye" it is usually "Slong"——So long!

ADIRONDACK WINTER FUN

The Adirondack winters were not long enough. The snow was deeper, the acres of firm, crusty snow were virtual air strips, the drifts were higher, and the wind-blown ice-covered ponds were like glass. There was lots to do and we did it.

We had a favorite hill for sleigh riding: steep enough to get a fast ride and just long enough for the return climb. We did not own it but it was ours. The owner never chased us off or worried about liability. A snow-packed jump in the middle added to the excitement. A few of the less-traveled roads also provided good sleigh riding. It was fun to attach fifteen or twenty American Flyers together and attain unheard-of speeds before wrecking up or reaching the bottom, whichever came first. And we had our moments of conquering the balance of the barrel stave.

Sleigh riding on a winter crust was a real treat. No need to break a trail, get snow down your neck, or walk up a hill. Just get on a sleigh and ride through the pasture lands. Steering was a bit treacherous and a little body drag was developed to retain control, not too good for the knees of your snowpants, however.

Snowfences abounded in the open fields along the Adirondack highways. They slowed the swirling snow and piled up the hills for sleighing or for digging snow caves. A snowdrift cave was warm and snug and the tightly packed snow provided a solid structure.

We had a couple choices for skating; put your skates on at the house and walk the half mile to the pond or go to the village rink. Usually the wind would blow the blue ice clear on the pond. The smooth mirror surface was perfect for fancy skating; our version was a lop-sided figure eight or trying to jump a barrel. Occasionally we had to shovel but it was part of the activity and all joined to make light work. The walk home was not without pain, though, the cold usually penetrated the skates and layers of socks and our toes suffered the consequences.

Our second skating choice was to put our skates over our shoulders and to walk the ten miles to Northville. (It was more like a mile and a half but as I get older the distance multiplies each time I tell the story.) The old skating rink was maintained on the little lake by the village and the portable skating house provided a warm place to change your skates and keep your feet from freezing. Retired trooper, Ed Blackmere, kept the wood fire going in the old barrel stove.

The village also owned a bobsled. It seated about twenty on a long board with foot rests on each side. It was our nearest experience to the world's greatest roller coaster. It took courage and some peer pressure. You took a seat near the middle, put your faith in the bigger boys on the front and back who handled the steering, and off you went. It was fast, no time for breathing, and usually over before you had time to think about jumping off. Too bad today's youth are bobsledless.

Downhill skiing was in its infancy in the early Adirondacks. It was rumored that somewhere they had hooked a rope to an old tractor and were pulling skiers up the hill. We did it the other way. Self tow! Our skiis were wooden and wide. They were held on with a leather toe strap. Each year we would secure an old tire inner tube from Elwin Tennant's garage and cut it into bands about an inch wide. They were just big enough to go around the circumference of a boot. The rubber band around the shoe and around the leather toe strap helped to keep the ski on while you went up and down the Adirondack hills. It was cross country skiing before it was invented. We used up endless Adirondack winter hours just moving from hill to hill in the mountains on our skiis.

Snowshoes were passed around among the Adirondack families. When someone got or made a new pair, the old ones were passed along to another. We usually had a few used pairs to strap on for a trip through the deep snows of the woods. It opened up woodlands that were impossible to reach by wading through the exhausting white stuff. Snowshoes were magic to us; the next best thing to walking on water. The stillness of the snow-draped wilderness was a mystery we relished. Hours of snowshoe hiking linked us to the other inhabitants of the winter woods; the rabbits, the deer, the winter birds and some of the lesser known furry creatures of the Adirondacks. And snowshoes got us in to the sugarbush to help with the sap gathering.

Sometime during the winter we managed to schedule in a few horse-drawn sleigh rides. One of the youth organizations from church or community would engage a horse and sleigh from a local farm and, loaded with hay and a good mixture of boys and girls, we would take a moonlight trip. There were those who liked to snuggle and those who liked to jump on and off the sleigh and to throw a little snow. It was good fun and usually ended with a hot cocoa party.

Adirondack toboggans were popular and usually someone had one or knew where to borrow one. (Remember Peters Toy Co.?) We loaded the toboggan with as many kids as possible and shot though the woods, dodging trees by leaning left or right. Unfortunately, we sometimes misjudged and had to roll off before a tree split the toboggan.

Winter in the Adirondacks was a busy time, too busy for cabin fever. Our winter sports and other pursuits kept us occupied during the long winter months and spring would interfere before we were ready to put away the sleigh, hang up the skates and snowshoes, and store the skiis and toboggan up in the barn.

ADIRONDACK SUMMER PLAYGROUND

It has been said that summer is boring. Some say there is "nothing to do." Not so in the days-gone-by. In the Adirondacks the summers were never long enough.

Our Adirondack summers were filled. There was always a week or two at summer camp, an extended visit to my grandparents' farm or to an aunt and uncle's, summer Bible school, attendance at parades and ballgames and, when older, a summer job.

Most of our other summer activities were self-manufactured. One of our major enterprises was fishing. It required picking night crawlers for bait. A rainy night on a good lawn brought out the big ones. A flashlite and a bucket used with a quick eye and hand would supply all the worms we needed and some to sell. When supplies ran short we mixed dry mustard with water and poured it down the worm holes. The hot mustard brought them to the surface in a hurry.

We knew the good fishing spots and usually used a hook and line tied to a fresh-cut sapling. Fancy gear was beyond our means and the fish tasted just as good caught on a wooden pole.

The woods supplied another avenue of summer fun. Sometimes we built a cabin or just climbed trees. We picked leeks and sorrel to eat. Hot summer days were best spent in the cool forest.

The Adirondack waters were our playground. We rode floating logs, dove off the boat docks, and slid down the rock-based mountain streams. We each had our favorite inner tube with too many patches to be used on the family car any more. Nothing better than to spend a lazy afternoon floating around an Adirondack pond in a rubber tube.

Brush haircuts and bare feet was the uniform of the summer. Getting the hair chopped off was not only cooler, it stayed out of your eyes when swimming and never needed combing. The bottoms of your feet turned into leather after a week or so and were tough enough for most activities. We just had to be careful where we stepped in the chicken yard.

Games filled the early evening hours. We usually rounded up enough people for a ball game. The "kick the can" version of hide-and-go-seek was a popular choice because we could keep the same person "it" for a long time. Shooting marbles and mumbletypeg were great pastimes on the lazy, hazy dogdays.

We still had chores to do. Cows, pigs, and chickens needed attention. Sometimes, someone in the Valley would get a horse and we would get a chance to ride. We often acquired wild pets such as frogs and turtles to care for. We were never without cats and dogs.

Berry picking was a never-ending pastime. We knew where to find the wild strawberries with a flavor lost to history. Our entire family picked blackberries off of the Adirondack hillsides. Blueberries and rhubarb found their way into pies and cakes. Raspberries, with a flavor all their own, were my favorites. Highbush cranberries and elderberries were more common than they are today. And our hedge row of billberry bushes provided a great place to hide as well as a berry good to eat.

Summer was indeed a busy time in the Adirondacks. I could add the time spent in the gardens, weeding and hoeing the corn and potatoes, the time spent helping the neighbors in one way or another, the time spent sitting around eating watermelon and spitting the seeds, and the endless hours just spent with good friends. Summer was never boring in the Adirondacks.

III

Adirondack Health

HEALTH-GIVING ADIRONDACKS

Modern man (and woman) underestimates the value of a wilderness experience. New York's Adirondack region, almost half "forever wild", lies in wait for each of us to take advantage of what our forefathers wisely saved for us. We, the people of New York State, own some 2.7 million acres of diverse Adirondack Country and we, the people, can secure the great potential it holds for us.

"Take a hike", when taken literally, holds great promise for those who penetrate the wilderness. And it does not have to be a lengthy, physically strenuous, wilderness trek. It can be tailor-made for the interested individual. The benefits are much the same at any level of accomplishment.

Many believe that the vast pine-covered Adirondack Mountains have health-giving features. The scent of pine in the air have purported to have healing features. Early Adirondack writer, the Reverend W. H. H. Murray, related stories of bedridden invalids going into the mountains and coming out the picture of health. Dr. Livingston Trudeau developed the curing process for tuberculoses in the Adirondacks. The Adirondacks have had their impact on stress, high blood pressure and nervous disorders for many over the years. A trip to the Adirondacks may be the best medicine a doctor can order.

Others have found religious peace in the Adirondack wilderness. Early writers speak of the great cathedral of the woods. The peace and solitude allow one's mind to clear and to become closer to God. Avowed atheist Adirondack hermit Noah Rondeau became a devoted Christian while spending his years away from civilization in the wilds of Cold River Country. Religious camps and retreats find the Adirondacks conducive to their work.

One thread weaves its way through the lives of history's greatest geniuses and producers. The value of a wilderness experience is common to each of them. They all speak of their time away from others when the mind clears and the problem is solved. Early writer, artists and philosophers had their camps in the Adirondacks. The wilderness experience helped to make them great.

You might begin your wilderness experience by taking one of two short forays into the Adirondack wilderness. One is called Auger or Olger Falls and the other is Jimmie Creek. They both require an auto trip to the Hamlet of Wells on Route 30 and beyond. It is a little over thirty miles north of Gloversville.

Olger Falls is reached by continuing beyond Wells on Route 30 toward Speculator. You pass the Wells Central School and the bridge across the Sacandaga River on Route 8. Drive up to the very top of the hill beyond the bridge (which is about three miles above Wells Village) and look for the International Paper Company parking lot and picnic area. A sharp U-turn off the main road will put you on the old macadam road going down to the Olger Falls trail. You can walk the short distance or drive it. There is a small drive-off for cars at the trail head.

The trail is marked on the trees with yellow trail markers and a twenty-minute, easy to moderate hike will take you to the falls. You will find the falls to your liking at any time of year. The spring runoff is violent and exciting. The summer meandering and steady surging is surprising. The winter ice and snow give it new beauty. They should charge admission! Taking the time to enjoy the misty falls will allow those negative ions to feed your brain and bring a new sense of peace to the daily stress.

Jimmie Creek provides the same experience. It is reached by crossing that three-mile bridge above Wells and going a short distance over Route 8. Watch for the creek, pronounced "crick," on the right side of the road. Park your car and take the short, short hike up the creek to the double falls. They can be enjoyed from the base or from the top of the small cliff which overhangs them. The perfect Adirondack grotto to bring a good feeling to your being.

Look to the Adirondacks for a renewed life. Like the old guide, spend so much time with those trees that, like the trees, you "grow some new wood each year."

THE HEALTHY ADIRONDACKS

Unfortunately, we are all guilty of not making full use of the great wilderness we have in the Adirondack region for our health. The health-giving features of the Adirondacks have long been known and volumes have been written about them. And today, the mountains are more accessible than ever, Yet, we live such busy, and sometimes unhealthy, lives that we ignore the opportunity they offer. Shame on us!

The Reverend W.H.H. Adirondack Murray espoused the healthy Adirondacks in 1869 in his book *Adventures in the Wilderness*. Dr. Edward L. Trudeau of TB fame wrote his story of "death-bed" to health in the Adirondacks in 1915. Melvil Dewey founded the Lake Placid Club for his health. Martha Reuben found her health in the Adirondacks and wrote *The Healing Woods* in 1952. And there were others who found health in the Adirondacks.

It must have been a venture of courage and risk to go to the Adirondack wilds in search of a "cure" in those early years. Many in the last stages of "consumption" desperately hunted for health in the forested Adirondacks. Those diagnosed with a case of "far-developed pulmonary phthisis" went to the mountains to regain their health, and they did. New York's great out-of-doors "healed the tubercular formations, rid the system of fever, checked the cough, put flesh on the wasted body, and strengthened the flabby muscles."

Back in the 1880's the journey to the healthy Adirondacks was not as easy as it is today. The train stopped at North Creek and the stagecoach ran forty miles through the wilderness up to Paul Smiths. Dr. Trudeau and Paul Smith had pioneered the way and others followed. Most came barely able to stand and walk, and within a year or two found themselves comparatively well.

Dr. A. L. Loomis of New York City read a paper before the State Medical Society in 1877 entitled, "The Adirondack Region as a Therapeutical Agent in the Treatment of Pulmonary Phthisis." It was printed in the Medical Journal and made everyone aware, along with physicians throughout the country, that the St. Regis country in the Adirondacks was a major contributor to a cure.

Dr. Loomis cites the climate, moist and cool, hot summer days with cool nights, and a winter of uninterrupted cold along with an air that is absolutely pure as the major contributors to the good results. The pine, balsam, spruce, and hemlock trees also create an atmosphere heavily laden with ozone. "The resinous odors of the evergreens benefit the diseased mucous membranes." Dr. Trudeau agreed from his own experience that the Adirondack Wilderness was far better for the sick than the climate found in any other state.

The "cure" could be taken in cottages, the sanitarium, or in tents in the Adirondacks. Those who chose tents found them unlike any camping experience that they had known. The tents were located on a lake with the evergreens around close to a hotel such as Paul Smiths. The breeze off the lake helped to keep the insects down.

Storerooms, dining tents, pantry, kitchen, and servants' quarters were all a part of the tent complex. Some were made of bark; others were large canvas tents. Excellent food was easily purchased from the hotel. The invalid's tent was equipped with a stove, a bedstead, wash stand, bookcase full of books, clock, field glasses, and some games.

Staying through the winter was an important part of the cure. The severe months were spent in the hotel or one of the cottages rather than in the tents. It was important, however, for the patients to get out into the fresh air each day; an idea frowned upon in the early medical practice when they were locked in a hot sick room with the shades drawn.

One record for the "cure" estimated the total cost in the 1880's as $480 for five months in the tent camp. Of that, $150 was for the Adirondack guide who also served as a nurse. Another $492 was spent on the hotel which included $84 to rent a horse for driving. A little over $900 or about $22 per week to recover from a fatal illness, not bad for an Adirondack cure!

SPRUCE GUM PICKIN'

A few years ago while prowling through an Adirondack antique shop (a great place to study the old Adirondacks), I found a small cardboard box with a picture of the mountains framed by a heart and surrounded by evergreen trees on it. The contents were labeled "DANIELS ADIRONDACK SPRUCE GUM." I had searched the woods for spruce gum and chewed it while growing up but had never experienced the store-bought kind.

The price was five cents. The ends of the box said that it "Sweetens the breath" and "Aids Digestion." The directions advised "Let this gum warm in the mouth before chewing." It went on to tout the medicinal purposes: "This gum is used by doctors. It is recommended for throat, lung and stomach troubles. It is also used by dentists. It is recommended for maintaining healthy gums and preservation of the teeth." The gum was collected in the Adirondacks and packaged by the Isaac Daniels Co. of Poland, New York.

Adirondackers were always looking for a way to bring in cash money and to stay healthy. In the 1880's spruce gum was growing in popularity. New Englanders had learned to chew the spruce tree pitch from the Native Americans and the Adirondackers had adopted the practice. Guides, farmers, and lumberjacks could pick three to ten pounds per day and receive eighty cents to a dollar fifty per pound. One champion spruce gum picker, Tim Crowley of Piseco, could gather sixty to one hundred pounds a day.

Ingenious Adirondackers developed their own methods of getting the spruce gum. Most picking was done in the early spring while the pitch was hard. Some collected during the slower months of winter when they were not so busy with other chores. A good Adirondack packbasket was used to transport the gum, keeping the hands free to cut it from the trees. A long pole was equipped with a knife blade; the picker could reach high up the trunk to get a wad of the gum. Oliver Whitman equipped his pole with a sharpened file, it worked better than a thin blade. A tin can was fastened to the pole below the blade and the gum would drop into the can. The can was emptied into the packbasket once it was filled. Some pickers would gouge the trees to let out the pitch so that the next trip would bring more gum.

The woodsmen enjoyed about a half century of good pickins' before modern technology entered the enterprise. Professionals were hired with steel climbing spurs and were paid five to six dollars a day to climb from limb to limb and tree to tree to increase the take. The gum was processed in factories so the pickers no longer had to spend long evening hours cleaning the dirt and bark out of the gum. However, factory-processed gum was not as well accepted as the old-fashioned hand picked variety and the industry died out.

The Adirondack Spruce Gum Company of Boonville hired a local buyer, Billy Stanyon, to purchase the gum from area pickers. He paid one dollar per pound for clear, clean gum and seventy-five cents per pound for not-so-clear gum. Others used the gum for barter in the local general store, "I went to the village and got the sack of flour that I paid for with gum". Once again, the bounty of the Adirondack wilds contributed to the subsistence of the Adirondack settlers.

ADIRONDACK GINSENG

How much would you pay for a root that gives a long healthy life while serving as an aphrodisiac, a root that lowers your blood pressure, lowers your blood sugar, serves as a tranquilizer, and keeps your brain running smoothly? The going price is over one hundred dollars a pound. The root is ginseng. And there is a ready market. Ginseng has been in demand for five thousand years and it continues to be a cash crop for Adirondackers today.

There are some records indicating that the five-leaf American ginseng was picked in the wilds of the Adirondacks as early as the eighteenth century. Some Adirondackers found the elusive plant on the north face of the tree-covered slopes while others favored the east side. Experienced ginseng pickers could locate the valuable plant whenever they needed cash money, although it was easiest to find in the fall when the seeds were scarlet and the leaves turned yellow-gold.

The name, ginseng, came from China, jin-chen, meaning "man-like." In the Adirondacks it is called "gingshang." Before the turn of the century Oliver Whitman recorded in his journals: "Oliver went gingshanging" and "George Thompson and Johney Thompson eat dinner hear [sic]. They had been gingshanging." He also recorded: "Mr. Kegg the gingshang man eat dinner hear [sic]." The buyers made the rounds in the Adirondacks and gave local pickers from five to thirty cents a pound for their ginseng roots.

Adirondack ginseng pickers always left three or more roots growing in the ginseng bed. Some took the time to remove the seeds and plant them in the forest floor. They knew that future digging depended on continuous growth. It takes three to four or more years for ginseng to reach sale size and it takes a big sack of dried roots to make a pound. The older and bigger, the better the price. Good Adirondack pickers can tell the age of the root by counting the little caps below the stem. Each year when it is killed by frost a new cap forms. The more the ginseng is shaped like a man the more it is worth. One man-like root in Russia is valued at $22,000.

Ginseng is used throughout the world. It is found in medicine, soap, lotions, chewing gum, hair tonic, wrinkle cream, bouillon, candy, shampoo, and tea. Adirondack ginseng is of high quality and the most desirable for export. The roots are of good size and shape and are generally considered the best for breeding stock although it is hard to cultivate. Adirondack ginseng was under protection and could not be exported during the '70's. Since then it has been intermittently under a non-export regulation. What other plant has an international control board watching over it?

There are those who laugh at the claims made by ginseng users. There are believers and non-believers. I knew an old Adirondack guide who dug ginseng most of his adult years and never had to worry about gray hair. When I referred to his use of ginseng he would just give me a knowing smile. He found it difficult to collect in his later years because of the ban against taking the plants from Forest Preserve lands. In some ways it is more difficult for today's Adirondackers to pursue those cash money activities such as ginseng digging than it was for the early Adirondack settlers.

Ginseng digging is not as easy as it may sound. It takes some doing to locate it in the hardwood forests of the Adirondacks. The plant must be identified and the roots carefully dug to get the most from the bed. There are plants that fool the novice. A few years ago a couple of Adirondack boys decided to make their fortune and took off to the mountains to dig ginseng root. They showed up in Broadalbin a few days later with two twenty-pound sacks of worthless roots. Others have been known to hide nails in the center of the roots to add to their weight; it caused buyers in the Orient to mistrust the American dealers. American dealers now give the ginseng the "magnet" test before buying.

Those who have not tried the world's most famous root do not know what they are missing. Taken by Russian cosmonauts, Olympic stars, Oriental rulers, and people of all nations, it continues to maintain its reputation as mankind's number one tonic. Adirondack ginseng may be just what you need.

SKUNK OIL

Adirondackers have known for years how to take care of those aches and pains associated with the rugged life in the mountains. Their relief was brought to them in a black and white package—the common skunk. Skunk oil is a true ointment; it will penetrate through three layers of skin and reach deep into the muscles and tendons. And, if you could take it, it would cure the common cold.

Skunk oil is made from the stomach fat of an Adirondack skunk. The old cook stove always had a pan of skunk fat sitting on the back, rendering out the valuable oil. It had to be carefully cooked down and bottled for future use. The skunk odor was faint because the fat of the animal is used to make the oil, not the smelly glands. Adirondack druggists mixed it with oil of wintergreen to give it a good flavor.

One of my uncles made skunk oil in the Adirondacks most of his life. He found a ready source of dead skunks along the Adirondack highways, especially on Sunday mornings since the slow-moving skunks were no match for the slow-thinking Saturday night drunks on their way home.

My uncle kept a plastic bag, a covered bucket, and a shovel in his car; you never knew when you might have to stop and pick up a skunk. In his early years, he trapped them during the season, usually October through December. The fall skunk has built up a good layer of stomach fat to get him through the winter.

Adirondack skunk oil collectors were wise in the ways of dealing with a skunk—even a dead one. They always removed their belts and wallets. Otherwise your friends would know when you were coming; the skunk smell will draw into the leather and stay. They also learned to remove the two smelly glands located between the hind legs. Accidentally cutting or breaking one during the process would provide an unwelcomed shower of smell. The hide of the skunk was carefully removed since it was another source of cash; hides were bringing three and a half dollars in 1918. Those with less white on them brought even higher prices.

During the skinning of the skunk the fat from the skin and body is saved. The entire layer of fat is cut out and put in the pan for rendering. The secret is to cook it slowly over a low fire to get out as much grease as possible without scorching. The grease is drained off during the frying; a scorched batch spoils the whole pot. The grease is strained through a cloth and bottled for future use or sale.

The medicinal uses for skunk oil were well-known by Adirondackers who lived far from doctors and hospitals. They not only used it for their own aches and pains, but used it on their horses. Mixed with beeswax it prevented lameness when rubbed on a horse's leg with a pine board. Mixed with turpentine and rubbed on the chest of a sick Adirondacker it would cure colds and congestion. Taking a spoonful now and then also helped to cure croup and cough.

Thus we find that the much-maligned skunk has a purpose on earth. This quiet, inoffensive animal, who prefers to avoid danger rather than seek it, not only goes about his business of eating harmful rodents and insects, but brings relief from aches and pains to the Adirondacker.

IV

Adirondack Industries

ADIRONDACK SUBSISTENCE

Life in the Adirondacks has always been tough; the rugged soil and unpredictable frost has defeated settlers from the day man first chose to settle New York's great wilderness. It is worth noting that there is no evidence that the native peoples ever made a permanent year-round settlement within the Adirondack Park. It was the settlers who arrived during the 1800's who attempted to tame the wilderness.

The lumbermen came and stripped the mountainsides, mining met with scattered success, and the wealthy set up their great wilderness "camps." A parallel activity, the growth of the Adirondack farms, was underway at the same time. As early as 1845 there were over three hundred farmers in the forested Hamilton County. Essex County had over three thousand farmers, Herkimer County over four thousand and Warren County had over two thousand farms. The other counties partially within the Blueline also had their share of farmers.

Farming in the Adirondacks consists of over fifty activities. There is no way an Adirondack family can subsist in the foreboding forests by simply doing one thing. Avocations become a part of the vocation. Woodworking, beekeeping, fishing, hunting, trapping, gathering, and preserving take their place along with a long list of other skills in the yearly cycle of life on an Adirondack farm.

The skills needed to keep a few animals, slaughter and preserve, grow and harvest food and grain, and to barter the surplus products, were passed from father to son and neighbor to neighbor in the early Adirondacks. Jackwax, maple candy, honey, pork tenderloin, salt pork, headcheese, and pickled pig hockies were among the staples in an Adirondack home.

Gathering the products of the wild consumed another portion of the Adirondacker's year. Berry picking, blackberries, bog cranberries, blueberries, and raspberries were the favorites while finding the butternut and beechnut trees, digging ginseng, and gathering spruce gum, leeks, and mushrooms took some learning. Most Adirondack family members, young and old, appreciated the importance of gathering to their family larder. And preserving foods involved the cutting of ice from an Adirondack pond, burying food in sand under the house, using a root cellar, as well as pickling and canning.

Wood has always been important to the Adirondacker. Cutting the supply to heat the house for the winter was a major task. Adding a sugarbush to their holdings increased the need for cutting firewood.

When it was time to build a house, barn, or other outbuilding, the timbers and boards came from the Adirondack forests. Each had to be selected, cut, peeled, hewed, and fitted. Wood parts for wagons and cutters were selected and cut, and put together with the help of the local blacksmith who created the metal parts.

Yoke and grain shovels were hand-carved and smoothed with the edge of a piece of glass. Native rustic furniture building was developed by the Adirondack farmers. Snowshoes were needed for winter travel. Some made dugouts or guideboats to traverse the Adirondack waters. Shingles were needed on all of the roofs. Tool handles were custom-made. Fish baskets and packbaskets were found in every home. Barrel hoop making brought in some cash from the cooper. And the list goes on.

Keeping the roads open fell to the overworked Adirondack farmer, who was required to maintain a section. Caring for sick animals and keeping the humans healthy was made difficult by the great distance to the nearest vet or physician.

Today's Adirondackers could take a lesson from the Adirondackers of yesteryears. Unemployment has become synonymous with the Adirondack region. With a little cooperation and some support from the state the economy of the Adirondacks, in my estimation, could take a turn for the better. An Adirondack Cooperative/Consortium including the public and the private sector could make the Adirondacks a profitable place to live.

Working through existing agencies such as DEC, Cooperative Extension, Soil Conservation and others, cooperatives, modeled after milk and produce cooperatives, could be set up and Adirondackers could become partners. Using a mentor/apprentice system appropriate Adirondack landowners with maple trees could start tapping. The sap could be picked up in tank trucks and taken to a central location in one of the hamlets for boiling into maple products. The same could be done with bee hives placed throughout the Adirondacks on the lands of cooperative Adirondackers. In the old days, neighbor taught neighbor and/or what one could do was shared with another.

Horse and buggy trips to selected Adirondack landmarks, such as is now being done at Santanoni, could be developed and promoted. Dog-sled rides have become popular throughout the nation; it would be a natural winter activity for many of the Adirondack loop trails. And how about a guideboat ride with a real Adirondack guide on an Adirondack lake; number one guide Pants Lawrence did it.

Using the wood of the forests to create finished products before it leaves the mountain is an idea whose time has come--again. It has the potential of creating profitable employment, which is the opposite of costly unemployment. The investment would be a wise one.

And maybe, just maybe, newly-trained spruce gum pickers and ginseng diggers could rejuvenate a once "cash money" practice in the Adirondacks. Fishing piers on the fish-filled Adirondack waters could be as profitable as the ocean fishing piers. A chain of "hunting camps," again, a public and private venture, would have multiple uses. There is a long tradition of opening Adirondack homes to travelers and a bed-and-breakfast business, with an Adirondack flavor, would attract a crowd of its own.

How about a giant Adirondack flea market specializing in Adiron-dack furniture and antiques and crafts and products of the forest? The same could be done with an Adirondack "Opry" featuring the Adiron-dack singers and story tellers.

The potential is present with the promotion of a partnership in the Adirondacks. Adirondackers, once known as "jacks of all trades," have an endless list of skills and offerings that would be a boon to New York's greatest asset. It is time to put them together in a cooperative venture that would benefit the Adirondack residents, and the citizens of our state, for years to come.

ADIRONDACK BOATBUILDING

When the early Adirondackers found out it was impossible to oper-ate a profitable farm in the mountainous wilderness they turned to other pursuits for making cash money. Three industries blossomed in the Adirondacks: hotel keeping, guiding, and boatbuilding. At one time or another, some one hundred thirty boatbuilders turned out lake boats and guideboats. A guideboat, unique to the Adirondack region, evolved to meet the need for a boat that could be rowed safely across an Adi-rondack lake and paddled up a mountain stream while carrying a guide, a sport, the gear, and bounty. It was not a canoe.

No one knows for certain who made the first guideboat. An Abeniki Indian, Mitchell Sabattis was one of the first. Others great names which appear among the styles and patterns of Adirondack guideboat building include Grant, Blanchard, Carey, Chase, Cole, Emerson, Hanmer, Martin, and Plumbley. Carl Hathaway of Saranac Lake is still building.

Another well-known boatbuilder was John P. Buyce of Speculator. John was a village blacksmith with a reputation as an expert horseshoer from Northville to Utica. He met the changing times by building boats to meet the demands of our nation's growing outdoor interests. He made lake boats for the tourists, cottage owners, fishermen, and camp owners. His guideboats were used by the hunters, fishermen, and guides.

John opened his shop in 1889 at the age of twenty and celebrated his fiftieth year in business in 1939. Similar to the other Adirondack boatbuilders, John developed his own style and design of boats. He improved on a lapstrake (clapboard) boat conceived and designed by his father, Fitch Buyce. He turned out twenty-five boats per year for seventy-five dollars apiece. With caned seats and mahogany they sold for a hundred and fifteen dollars. Today they would bring over five thousand dollars.

John Buyce's boats cost a little more to make but he insisted upon quality and excellence. His guideboats were a foot shorter than his lake boats, usually twelve to fourteen feet in length. They weighed around fifty pounds. The spruce knees and oars were made of native Adirondack wood while the bottom of cypress, sides and deck of cedar and gunnels of oak were made of wood ordered and shipped in from other parts. Adirondack boatbuilders were true craftsmen, the boats demanded it.

The insistence on quality paid off. During World War II, when the allies were making the drive to the German heartland, a Buyce boat was spotted and used to cross the Rhine River by Ed Brooks of Lake Pleasant. John put a nameplate on each of his boats. And Buyce boats are still in use today.

John Buyce also had a special friendship with Lake Pleasant hermit guide, French Louie. It was general knowledge that when French Louie made his semiannual trip out of the woods to Speculator he would spend all of his hunting and trapping profits in one big, week-long fling. Not true! John would get a visit from Louie before the old hermit began his serious drinking. Louie would entrust some of his earnings to

John for safekeeping. According to John, at times he had as much as five hundred of Louie's dollars in his safe.

Typical of true Adirondackers, John did not solely depend on boatbuilding to eke out an Adirondack livelihood. He built wooden snowplows, cutters, buckboards, lumber wagons, and log haulers. He served six years as town clerk, six years as mayor, and ten years as town supervisor. He was a member of the Winter Sports Club Committee in the '20's which brought winter sports to Speculator. And we thought we were busy!

Boatbuilders are few and far between in today's Adirondacks but the need for one of the Adirondack's first industries is still here. Antique guideboats demand a good price and today's guideboats from within and without the Adirondacks remain at top market value. Apparently, the early Adirondack boatbuilders, such as John Buyce, knew a good product and developed it to perfection. The traditional craft of the Adirondack waters will be with us for times to come, yet, you will not find the name of this unique Adirondack boat in any dictionary!

ADIRONDACK FURNITURE

"I'm going out in the woods and cut some new furniture," could have been heard in an Adirondack home at the turn of the century. Adirondack craftsmen had learned how to fashion rustic furniture from the native material growing on the Adirondack hillsides. And the growth of Adirondack camps and hotels created a demand for furniture indigenous to the region.

Adirondack furniture makers were widespread throughout the mountains. Distance influenced their creativity; there was no opportunity to copy one another. Varied methods and designs were the results of the distance factor in the Mountains. The exclusive use of native materials was about the only commonality among the builders. In many cases, the unique curve or growth of the wood determined the design.

Birch was a popular wood for some of the Adirondack furniture makers. It fit well with the practical, sturdy look of the backwoodsman. They built sturdy furniture and some is still in use today, bringing high prices from the collectors and wealthy camp owners.

One Such Adirondack craftsman was Lee Fountain who made Adirondack birch furniture at "Whitehouse" near Wells. Remember when the Northville-Lake Placid trail guide suggested, "call across the West Branch of the Sacandaga River to the white house for a boat." That's the place. Lee Fountain operated a lodge and cabin business at the Whitehouse until the late 1940's.

Lee was a true Adirondaker. He spent many off-season hours fashioning his style of Adirondack furniture. Local farmers could also supplement their income by spending a few weeks assisting with the wood gathering and making ash caning strips.

Lee cut his birch at the proper time of year. In the late fall, just before snowfall, after the major harvesting was finished, time was available to search out an Adirondack hillside to cut a supply of the proper size birch. The leaves were off the trees and the sap had stopped for the dormant stage of winter. The conditions were just right and the bark would tighten and last forever. Lee left his furniture in its native state without coating it with varnish or shellac.

Lee's giant birch-stump tables are a work of art. The base of stump was carefully chosen for its shape and balance. Once cut and brought in from the woods it was placed in a giant sap pan of water. When lifted out it was cut at the waterline around the bottom. This method of leveling provided a flat base so the table would set level on the floor. The table top was then ringed with small birch twigs patiently nailed on by the maker. My table has one hundred twenty of them.

The Fountain's rocking chairs are also reflective of the art of Adirondack furniture making. The curved legs on the front pieces were obtained from a special spot on the Adirondack hillsides where the trees grew out and up to the light in a natural curve.

Lee also fashioned rustic porch swings, lamp stands, clothes racks, tea carts, desks, stools, and regular chairs. His unique designs and careful craftsmanship created furniture still in use today. Samples may be seen in the Adirondack Museum. And, if imitation is the greatest form of flattery, Lee can be flattered. Today's Adirondack furniture makers are carrying on the great tradition of rustic furniture making, keeping Lee's craftsmanship alive.

THE ADIRONDACK PACKBASKET

If man ever loved an inanimate object it was his Adirondack packbasket. A lifetime of adventure and history can be shared with a good basket and all those memories are recollected each time the old pack-basket is brought out. Some become family heirlooms.

The ash-splint packbasket has been around a long time and some trace its origin to the Adirondacks. Look at the oldest picture that you can find of man in the Adirondacks and you will find a packbasket sitting in the background. When man entered the woods the packbasket went with him.

Trappers, who sought the bounty of the Adirondacks, needed a conveyance to carry the hides. The packbasket was just the thing for traps and hides. It had ample room and protected the contents. Strapped to the back with shoulder straps, the arms were left free to carry a gun or hiking staff.

Loggers trucked tons of food to the lumber camps. Their "trucks" were Adirondack packbaskets. Loaded with salt pork, flour, potatoes, and other camp fare they ensured the giant meals consumed by the hungry lumberjacks.

Packbaskets are not as comfortable to some as today's nylon packs and packbaskets are not entirely waterproof, yet, they were accepted and used for decades in the Adirondacks. My own packbasket is over forty years old, has carried each of our five children, and all my camping gear for decades. A good pack basket lasts as long as its owner and beyond.

The early packbaskets were made by the guides and Native Americans who used them. The craft was taken up by others and baskets were made to sell. Dan Emmett, the Indian, taught hermit Noah Rondeau how to make them. A band of gypsies traveled the Adirondacks at one time, camped near the villages, and made packbaskets to sell. They stayed as long as the market required.

One of the last packbasket makers of note was Andrew Joseph. Andrew was born in an Abenaki Indian encampment of the Algonquin Nation at Saratoga Springs in 1892. He was talked into settling at Long Lake by his cousin, Mitchell Sabattis, where he became a well-known Adirondack guide and craftsman. He was called "the old work horse of the woods."

Mohawk Indian ladies are also carrying on the packbasket tradition. They can be seen at their gatherings still making baskets in the old way; imbedding a knife in a stump and drawing the splints through the blade using an experienced eye to maintain a uniform width.

It takes work to make a good Adirondack packbasket. An ash log needed to be stripped of its bark. The inner wood was then pounded loose with a mallet and pulled off in splints. The splints had to be cut to uniform width and thickness, usually by the "eye method" through the sharp blade. Weaving the basket to the desired shape and size challenged the craftsman. Some were made like bushel baskets to carry the bulky loads and others were narrowed at the top to protect the personal gear inside. Preserving the wood with a mixture of turpentine and linseed oil finished the job.

Adirondack pack baskets are still available and used today. Craftsmen such as Bill Smith of Colton carry on the tradition. There are some who follow the traditional models with well-cut splints and wooden handgrips on the top and there are those mass-produced with nylon handles. Choose your Adirondack packbasket well and it will be your wilderness "truck" for a lifetime.

SUGARIN' OFF IN THE ADIRONDACKS

The days get longer. The combination of cold nights and warm days provides the stimulus for the sap to run. Spring comes to the snow-covered Adirondacks and the giant sugar maples stand ready for the annual spring ritual—sugaring off.

"Sugaring off," the gathering and boiling of the maple sap into syrup and sugar, requires the chopping and cutting of cords of firewood. It requires snowshoeing through miles of soft snow to drill the trees. Hundreds of sap spiles made by hand from sumac twigs are tapped into the holes and hung with sap buckets. A temporary lean-to covered with a layer of evergreen branches is erected for a windbreak and lunchroom. The giant pan is set on rocks or a giant sap kettle is hung on a pole and a hot fire is coaxed into being underneath. And the annual boiling of the maple sap begins.

The Adirondacks has had, and now has, its share of sugarbushes, those special places where the sap of the giant Adirondack sugar maple trees is boiled down until it reaches the consistency of sweet and tasty maple syrup or maple sugar. Henry Girard had the largest sugarbush in the southern Adirondacks near Griffin on Route 8. He tapped fifteen thousand trees. It required keeping the woods roads open all winter, so that he could tap the trees in February. The sap starts flowing in March, or some years in February or as late as April, depending on Mother Nature. Henry's gathering tanks held six barrels of the raw sap. It took seven teams and twenty-five men to make the two hundred fifty gallons of syrup per day.

Seth Low operated a fifty thousand-tree sugarbush near Sabattis. He had over sixty thousand buckets and five sugarhouses. He put in railroad tracks and purchased three used locomotives to transport the sap through the thirty-six-square-mile bush when the snow was soft. The sugarbush was a year-round operation with maintenance and the summertime candy and sugar cake making. The entire business was lost in the forest fire of 1903.

Adirondack towns listed maple sugar production as a major industry for several decades beginning around the middle of the 19th century. As early as 1840, Hamilton County produced over thirty-five thousand pounds of sugar. Twenty-five years later they were still recording over twenty-five thousand pounds per year and five hundred gallons of maple molasses, as it was called in the old days.

Most Adirondack settlers quickly learned to add maple sugar production to their cash money activities. It was a source of ready cash during the slow time of the year. On March 29, 1897, Oliver Whitman recorded in his Westhill Journals the tapping of ninety-five trees. On March 30 he tapped another sixty-five trees. The next day they finished tapping the sugarbush. On April 1, Oliver boiled down the sap to get two buckets of syrup. Five days later he recorded one hundred fifty pounds of sugar "made so far this spring."

It takes thirty-five to forty gallons of sap to make a gallon of syrup and the average tree is good for twenty-five gallons of sap per season. Syrup is boiled down further to make maple sugar, thus, it takes a lot of sap to run a sugarbush. It was a tradition among the early Adirondackers to never drink the raw sap; it reportedly was inclined to be "very weak'nin." Apparently, the story was told to keep the hired help from drinking out of the sap buckets.

The Whitmans made "sixty pounds of sugar and two gallons of molassas" during the week of April 15. On April 19 the sap was used to make vinegar, a good use of the late-in-the-season sap .

One of the tastiest uses of maple sap is to make "jackwax." The syrup is boiled to a thick consistency that coagulates when dipped onto a pan of clean snow. A whittled maple twig or fork is used to roll up some of the sticky, height-of-sweetness candy to eat. Jim Rieth kept a teapot of syrup on his sugarbush stove in Bleecker ready to pour out for jackwax at any time. He also boiled eggs in the hot, sweet sap and washed them down with a cup of sweet sap instant coffee.

Jackwax parties were a popular form of fund-raising in Adirondack communities, much as church suppers are today. One needed to exercise some caution, however, as too much of the sweet maple product could take its toll. The girls club of Wells visited Jim Hosley's sugar camp on April 1, 1910 and ate their fill of jackwax, hot sugar, and maple syrup. School attendance was irregular the following week and Dr. Head reported that he wore out his stomach pumps and had prescribed all the pills he could muster.

Thus we find that the stately maples that bring color and beauty to our Adirondack mountainsides are also a part of the economy of the Adirondack settlements.

LUMBERING THE ADIRONDACKS

Years ago we took an old truck, drove over a long muddy woods road to Mud Lake. There we loaded up slabs from the sawmill. They were the waste and bark pieces from the sawing of the lumber and were free for the taking. Split and piled they make great firewood and kept us warm all winter. The wood of the Adirondacks has long been a part of the lives of its inhabitants.

Lumbering came to the Adirondacks with the settlers. Lumber was a basic need in building the houses and farm buildings. The first mills were set up, usually by the first settler, for individual needs. It was not long before the man with the sawmill was sought out by new neighbors. Land had to be cleared for farming and the logs had to be removed. Homes had to be heated and kilns for plaster had to be fired. Wood was a vital part of the lives of the people. Our nation was growing and the trees of the Adirondacks were in great demand.

Lumbering got off to a good start in New York's Adirondacks in the 1700's. The early mills were in the mountain foothills of Warren, Essex, Herkimer, and Fulton counties. One of the earliest mills of record was erected in 1764 near Queensbury in Warren County by Moses Clements. Essex County had a mill at Willsborough in 1767 operated by the founder of the settlement, William Guilliland. Sir William Johnson built his first mill in the Adirondacks in 1773 near Mayfield.

Other mills sprang up where settlers were building their homes.

Herkimer County gained their first mill in 1776 in a settlement at Stark by Abraham Van Horne. An early mill was erected at Hadley in 1791 by Delane and Hazard. Lake Pleasant in Hamilton County got a mill in 1795. It was built by Thomas Foster. One can see that in those days "we took the sawmills to the logs; today we take the logs to the sawmills."

The tall, straight white pines became in great demand for ship masts and were the first to go. Spruce was cut for pulp. These giant white pines and red spruce, so plentiful in the Adirondacks, appeared to be in endless supply. By 1813 the lumbermen moved from the foothills into the mountains and by the middle of the century they were well into the central Adirondacks. The move into the deeper mountains was made possible by the development of river transportation for moving logs.

The idea for floating logs on the rivers was originated and was first used down the Schroon River to the Hudson for the mills at Glens Falls. Thus, the Adirondacks became the source of a new method of transporting logs and the waterways of the Adirondacks were legally declared "public highways." "Highway improvements" in 1854 included five thousand dollars spent on the Sacandaga River to clear the channel near Fish House and clearing the West Branch to Arietta and the East Branch through Wells to Lake Pleasant.

The last half of the nineteenth century marked increased growth in the Adirondack lumber industry. Clear cutting of the Adirondack mountainsides began. Loggers were forced to brand their logs with a unique design to mark them as they went down the rivers to the mills. A special hammer was used to hit the end of each log with the design such as a crow's foot, double O, deer's foot, heart, etc. The heart identified the Morgan Lumber Company later to become the International Paper Company. Finch, Pruyn used a fancy L crossed like an F.

In 1872 a drive of two hundred million feet of logs was counted at Glens Falls, most of which came out of the forests of Hamilton County. Loggers, at that time, were cutting "two-log trees" when "market" trees were nineteen inches in diameter on the small end and thirteen feet long. No one knows why logs in the Adirondack forests were standardized at thirteen feet when the rest of the country was at sixteen feet. Possibly it was an original twelve-foot log with an extra foot for good measure. One logger was cutting about one hundred softwood logs per day. These logs were simply sold by count in the Adirondacks; other places were using the accepted Doyle or Scribner measurements.

Logging camps were found throughout the Adirondacks. They consisted of log buildings with dirt floors. The walls were well-chinked with sticks and moss to keep out the wind and cold. One long, low building consisted of an attic of bunks and a ground floor for the kitchen and dining hall. One end was a "men's room" for evening activities. The crew spent their evenings smoking, reading, singing, and card playing. Crews were not allowed in the dining halls or kitchen except during mealtime.

When women were eventually allowed into the camps as cooks, a dipperful of hot water kept "snoopers" away from the kitchen. The camp also had another one story building for a horse barn and the indispensable blacksmith usually had a small shop. An office was sometimes built for the boss, the log scaler, the timekeeper, and for a small company store of necessities.

During the winter cutting of logs, icy hillsides were a problem. Roads were made by compacting the snow and spraying it with water. Straw and hay on the slippery roads helped to slow the horses taking the heavy loads to the waterways. Special brakes were designed and ropes were used. Some of the men served as sand spreaders. As the load came down off the mountain the driver would shout "more sand" trusting that today's sand spreader was not someone he had had a fight with the previous day.

Logging has always been a dangerous occupation. "Widow makers," dead branches which drop on the head of the unsuspecting logger and trees kicking out or falling while being chopped took their toll. The river drivers who rode the logs down the fast-flowing spring waterways risked their lives every day.

The days were long in the woods. It was not unusual to eat breakfast at three A.M. and work to dark. The urgency to get the logs out and ready for spring thaw motivated the speed of work. Some unscrupulous bosses were known to set the clocks ahead to fool the help. One was told that if he kept setting the clock so far ahead, "it will be the Fourth of July before the snow goes off."

It has been years since we went to Mud Lake for free wood, yet nothing has really changed in the Adirondack lumber business. The tools are better but the loggers still go after those giant trees, mills still prepare them for market, and we still enjoy a world made of Adirondack wood.

V

Adirondack Animals

TALK TO THE ANIMALS

Adirondackers have been talking to the animals since the days of the mighty hunters Nick Stoner and John Cheney. At a time when the Adirondack settlers depended upon the bounty of the forest to feed their families, the skilled hunter used his wiles to increase the success of the hunt. They included talking to the animals.

Animals have their own language. The Adirondack moose of yesteryears, and I suppose those who are moving back today, had a language composed of sighs, grunts, groans, howls, and roars. Hunters took note of the moose communication and joined in. They learned that grunting when you ought to howl or roaring before the groan were grammatical errors if you wanted to communicate with a moose.

A good moose caller needed a horn; the human voice cannot duplicate a moose without help. A true moose horn must be made out of selected birch bark. Not every specimen of birch bark will give the proper ring and experienced moose callers can detect the difference.

The Adirondackers fashioned their moose horns around a cone of wood eighteen to twenty-two inches long and four to six inches at the base. The point of the cone is cut off where the cone is about one inch in diameter. The birch bark is soaked in warm water and wrapped around the cone to a thickness of about one-eighth an inch. It is tied on and left to set. It is then removed and sewn with twine along the seam using an awl and then the ends are trimmed. It has become one of today's most sought after Adirondack antiques.

It takes years to master the art of moose calling; the successful sound must come from the caller's throat. It begins with a groaning "err" and then is drawn out at length, gradually turning into a roar and a howl, and then dying away. The sound is repeated three times with a variety of force and inflection. And all this is done while rotating the horn in a figure eight.

Turkey talk was not quite as complicated as moose talk. Hunters talked to the turkeys by rubbing two cedar sticks together to imitate the turkey language. A higher class version required a corn cob on the end of a cedar stick. Rubbing the opposite end against a piece of slate resulted in a call irresistible to the wild birds. Some hunters used the turkey against himself by blowing on a turkey wing bone to make a turkey noise.

Some Adirondack squirrel hunters learned to play on their natural curiosity. While walking through the woods they would make a chipping noise with their teeth, tongue and lips. The sound was similar to normal squirrel talk and quickly brought them out to say "hello."

Did you ever carry on a conversation with an Adirondack deer? It is an exercise in futility; they are good listeners but not great talkers. This majestic creature of the forest has learned to be less than communicative. I would characterize the Adirondack buck as the strong, silent type. They may bleat when injured or terrified, but that is a rarity. Most often you may find that the buck is a grunter, usually when in full rut. Their offspring may be heard bleating for their mothers but they soon learn to lie quietly until danger goes away.

Adirondackers have found over the years that you can talk with the deer in different ways. A deer will often show himself when you make a squeaky sound; between the lips much as you do to make a baby laugh. Sometimes a soft whistle will attract a curious deer. The best method, however, is to rattle the antlers.

Deer respond to the sound of another deer rattling his antlers. Most call it "horn rattling" although antlers are used to imitate the rutting deer. Scraping antlers together, scratching in the leaves, or rubbing them on a tree can be used to attract an Adirondack buck. It is an art that places the human in direct communication with an elusive creature of the wild.

The Adirondack black bear is another story. The way to the wary bear is through his stomach. Do not waste words, send him a message that reaches his hungry nose.

THE LAST ADIRONDACK MOOSE

Recommendation number 69 under the Wildlife section of the Report of the Temporary Study Commission on the Future of the Adirondacks written in 1971 made a bold suggestion: "Extirpated native species should be reintroduced wherever appropriate stock is available and the potential for a successful restocking is considered good." One-time residents missing from the Adirondacks include the lynx, wolverine, wolf, and puma. And one of the greatest of the extirpated (missing) species is the moose.

The moose was once a common Adirondack mammal that enjoyed a good life in the mature forests of the mountains. Logging expanded the deer range and a parasite associated with the deer was fatal to the moose. The accuracy of the early hunters probably helped to finish off the Adirondack moose.

Alvah Dunning and his father took three or four moose a day, and occasionally five a day. Alvah said that they "petered out" during the winter of 1854-55. The end of the Adirondack moose was rather abrupt; only scattered reports were recorded after the 1850's.

The sighting or taking of the last moose in the Adirondacks has been debated for years. The last moose in the Griffin area of Hamilton County was reported in 1852. The fourteen-year-old son of Phillip and Abby Wadsworth was out in the woods with his dogs. The dogs drove a moose into the Sacandaga River near Big Bear Brook. The boy was so frightened by the big antlers that he hid in the dry bed of the creek until the animal left.

New York Governor Horatio Seymour thought that he took the last moose. Hunting near Jocks Lake in Herkimer County in 1859 he took a big one.

Another party of hunters claimed the "last moose" in the Adirondacks. Four men from Philadelphia hunting with physician-turned-guide, Captain Calvin Palmer of Long Lake, spotted a moose near the east inlet of Raquette Lake. It took four shots to bring down the magnificent animal. It stood seven feet tall at the hump and weighed eight hundred pounds. Most historians call this the last Adirondack moose.

Alvah Dunning deserves the honor of claiming the last moose. Hunting near West Canada Creek in March of 1862, Alvah took his last moose. It was verified by *Field and Stream* magazine. Some still say that it happened in 1860, but if Alvah is right about 1862, he was the last of the old-time moose hunters in the Adirondacks.

Attempts to reintroduce the moose to the Adirondacks have been made over the years. Wealthy landowners put up fences and imported the moose only to have them escape and fall prey to the poachers.

In 1902, eight moose were brought from Canada and released in the Adirondacks. Four more were added the next year. It cost three thousand dollars and met with failure. The Browns Tract Guides had raised five thousand dollars in 1901 to help reinstate the Adirondack moose.

Scattered reports of moose in the Adirondacks continues to this day. Verplanck Colvin, the state surveyor, reported signs of Adirondack moose as late as 1874 in some of the most remote spots in the mountains. A transient cow moose made a tour of the northeastern Adirondacks in 1957. A young bull was shot by a hunter in 1962 in the Adirondacks. Apparently the moose were trying to return to the mountains in spite of man's failure to reintroduce them.

Beginning in the 1980's the moose have immigrated from east and north of New York State to the Adirondack Mountains. Seven moved in during the early '80's and have now expanded to over twenty animals. And they have decided to stay in the Adirondacks. Now we have to decide if we welcome these original residents back in their homeland.

THE ADIRONDACK BLACK BEAR

Back in the roaring '20's no one had to worry about the Adirondack black bear. The population was estimated to be around one thousand one hundred for New York State with the great majority of the bear in the Adirondack counties. Hunters accounted for less than two hundred bear per year. Few were sighted and plans were made so that "...this exceedingly interesting and largely inoffensive creature may be assured of a permanent place in our fauna."

It worked, whatever it was. The Adirondack black bear has made a big comeback. Those who camp and hunt in the Adirondacks continue to have sightings of the bear. The Adirondack dumps and camp garbage quickly attract the hungry creatures. They can smell a candy bar in the bottom of your pack inside a tent or cabin. Some say that there are too many bear in the Adirondacks.

Today's bear population in the Adirondacks is approaching four thousand. Hunters took over six hundred during the latest season in the mountains. Most bear taken were around five years old with one bear over forty-two years old taken in Essex County the year before.

The bear are a vibrant part of Adirondack history. Man is their only predator. Although there is no recorded case of a black bear killing a human in the Adirondacks, there have been some maulings and scares. Mart Moody used to tell the story of how two bear blocked him from both openings in a crevice and they "et me up, of course!"

The Adirondack black bear was a great entertainer. The small tanning villages such as Griffin welcomed the old hunter who came to town on Saturday night with his tame dancing bear. It was a sight to behold.

Oliver H. Whitman supplied Sacandaga Park, the Gem of the Adirondacks resort near Northville, with the bear for their tourist attractions. Some escaped from the cage and were shot. On other occasions, Oliver was called to the Park to recapture one of his bears. It was not uncommon for Oliver or one of the Adirondack farmers to have a bear in a pen for visitors to see.

The *Hamilton County Record* newspaper reported on a bear in February of 1900. Harry Paige of Sacandaga Park owned a bear for a pet. He dug a hole for the bears den and built a hut over it. The bear tore the hut down and built his own den.

On Ground Hog's Day a big crowd gathered to see the bear come out of his den. They wanted to see "if the Candlemas Day tradition was true." Apparently it was not; the bear never came out until February 15 and he went right back in to stay another month or two. Some either confused the bear with a groundhog (woodchuck) or, the "see your shadow" tradition applied to any hibernating animal.

There have been other "famous" Adirondack black bears. Hermit-guide Bob Glassbrook had a card-playing bear but had to shoot him when he caught him cheating. On another occasion Bob accused a couple of hunters of killing a bear that helped him with his spring plowing.

One of the Smith boys, protecting their hogs on their remote farm near Griffin, shot "at least three bear" near the pigpen. When help was summoned to retrieve the animals, for some unknown reason, only one bear was found!

The Adirondack black bear are facing a new danger today. Unscrupulous poachers are after the bear for various organs which sell for high prices on the overseas market. Our special relationship with the Adirondacks' biggest game animal gives us added responsibility for his welfare—"that he might be assured of a permanent place in our fauna."

ADIRONDACK 'SKEETERS

One Adirondack hermit observed that there were "twenty-six varieties of punkies, blackflies, deer flies, and mosquitoes along with yellow jackets, hornets, wasps, and houseflies, and yellow ants, carpenter ants and body mites, headlice and fleas in the Adirondacks." Give or take a few in either direction and everyone will agree that there are enough of 'em to be "pesky"! And those who give us the most friendly attention are those giant, blood-sucking Adirondack mosquitoes.

Do not confuse the mosquitoes with the blackflies and punkies (no-see-ums). Those two are bad enough but they do not compare with the female of the mosquito species. Blackflies emerge in the spring to swarm around your head for a month and to fill your eyes, nose, and ears with their tiny black bodies. The blackfly female needs a good meal of blood to fly up the swift streams to lay her eggs in the smaller, swifter tributaries. The one consolation is that they will usually be gone by early July in the Adirondacks.

We always called the no-see-ums punkies. It came from the Algonquin Indians, punki, which meant piercing and sucking mouth parts. Apparently the little pests also kept the Native Americans from enjoying the Adirondacks. I thought the term came from "punk" which is someone who is worthless. Punkies come from the midge family and like to bite. Their tiny bodies, somewhat transparent, make them, at times, a formidable foe in the wilds of the Adirondacks.

Mosquitoes are the ones who test man's ingenuity. The female requires blood as part of the life cycle. She searches out man or animal, day or night, to get a drink. Unfortunately when she drinks she leaves an itchy welt behind. The reaction is caused by the chemistry of her saliva.

Early Adirondackers combated the mosquito with the smudge. A fire was built and then smothered with wet forest debris to fill the air with smoke. Mosquitoes did not like the smoke and left the scene. Unfortunately, the humans were left to cough and spit in a cloud of unhealthy smoke.

Other Adirondackers resorted to science A boiled mixture of pine tar, castor oil, and pennyroyal (3:2:1) was rubbed on all exposed parts of the body. It kept the mosquitoes off but left a mess on the one who used it. Local druggists made a supply for those who chose to purchase it ready-made thus initiating today's lucrative repellant industry.

One Adirondack family took to the water. Blackflies and mosquitoes rarely venture to the middle of the Adirondack lakes in search of sustenance, thus one finds a haven during the height of the season. It works especially well for the springtime blackfly influx.

The Durant family, owners of Pine Knot Great Camp on Raquette Lake, built a houseboat. Named *The Barque of Pine Knot*, the Swiss chalet-style home on the water was elegant. It contained three rooms along with a kitchen and bath. It was fully operable with running water. The interior is wainscoted and highly polished; there is nothing like escaping the pesty scourge in comfort and style. The *Barque* is now a museum on the grounds of Cortland College's Camp Fine Knot campus at Raquette Lake.

Another Adirondacker literally took to the water. French Louie spent many an Adirondack night sleeping in the swamp. He found that sinking his body in an Adirondack swamp with just his nose sticking out kept the pesty mosquitoes from their dirty work. He had learned from the animals that submerging in water truly spelled relief.

There are a couple things you should know about Adirondack mosquitoes. First of all, Guide Paul Smith said they are smart flies, "They eat the outsiders first and save the natives for later." It pays to be born and raised in the Adirondacks. Lucky for me, the mosquitoes are still saving me for later; the chemistry of my body signals to them that I am a seventh generation native.

Adirondack mosquitoes love blue. Their small brains tell them that the blue is the sky or water and it attracts them. Some of them are also attracted to bright colors, much as they are attracted to light at night. Leave your blue and bright fashions at home when you go to the Adirondacks.

The old guides wore their protection. Their unique hats, although varied in kind and style, were designed for bug protection. Most had a turned-up brim to keep the sweat off their brows and an extended brim on the opposite side to be rotated to keep the sun out of their eyes or the rain off the back of their necks. The old guides explained, "with this hat the skeeters can't ketch up with me, they don't know if I'm a comin' or a going!" And, if the hat smelled bad enough, it chased away the mosquitoes anyway.

Nature has not abandoned the Adirondacks completely. The wet spots in the woods grow a useful plant called jewelweed. It has an orange blossom and when the leaves are held under water they sparkle like diamonds. The hollow stems are filled with a liquid that neutralizes the mosquito saliva. Rubbed on a fresh bite the itching stops. Jewelweed is also called Touch Me Not; an appropriate message for the pesky creatures. It is a good plant to know if you like to be in the woods.

When all else fails, smile and accept the little creatures. Modern science will someday get beyond Skin-so-Soft. And a final word for those who suffer from bug bites: the Old Guide says the best way to prevent infection caused by biting insects is "don't bite any!"

VI

Adirondack Protection

FOREVER WILD—THE PEOPLE'S CHOICE

New Yorkers have chosen to keep the Adirondacks "forever wild." It was placed in the New York State Constitution in the 1894 General Election voting as Article VII and has remained there ever since. It was recoded in the Constitutional Convention to become Article XIV but was left "forever wild." The original language approved by the voters almost 100 years ago remains the same:

> "The lands of the State, now owned or hereafter acquired, constituting the forest preserve as now fixed by law, shall be forever kept as wild forest lands. They shall not be leased, sold or exchanged, or be taken by any corporation, public or private, nor shall the timber thereon be sold, removed or destroyed."

Whenever a need arises to make a change in the "forever wild" provision the voters must make the choice. It has happened over one hundred fifty times since 1894. Although these changes have been introduced in the Legislature, only twenty-seven of them have reached the voters at the polls. The voters have agreed to nineteen amendments to Article XIV. It is not an easy job to change the special protection given to our State's crown jewels, the Adirondacks.

The protection given to the Adirondacks was the result of the lenient administration of the State lands. Timber was being sold, sometimes in questionable deals. Some lands were sold. Leases were offered on five acre lots on the Preserve. The voters did not like what was happening and choose to put solid protection right in the Constitution of the State. It became effective on January 1, 1855.

The amendments followed. The voters rejected a move to allow the leases and sale of lands to continue in 1896. The voters rejected a new Constitution in 1915 'which included reforestation, building of fire trails, removal of dead trees, and a highway from Saranac Lake to Old Forge. The 1923 voters defeated a proposal for hydroelectric power on State lands. A proposal to construct additional paths, trails, campsites, and cabins was rejected in 1932. The 1953 voters blocked the Moose River dam project and the 1955 voters did the same to the Panther Mountain Reservoir proposal.

Other projects fell under the axe of the State's citizens. A relocating of Route 10 in Arietta was defeated in 1961. The 1967 Constitutional Convention reworded the "forever wild" protection and the voters turned it down at the 1967 General Election.

The owners (us) of New York's Forest Preserve have voted in favor of some of the special requests for waiving of the "forever wild" provision in the Adirondacks. In 1913 up to three percent of the total acreage was approved for water supply, canals, and to regulate the flow of streams. The flow of streams was removed in 1953 to prevent additional dams. State highways were approved in 1918 from Saranac Lake to Tupper Lake (Route 3) to Blue Mountain Lake (Route 30) and to Old Forge (Route 28). The Whiteface Mountain Highway was added in 1927 and the Indian Lake to Speculator (Route 30) was constructed in 1933. The Adirondack Northway got some Preserve lands in 1959.

Construction on Adirondack Preserve lands has come before the voters. In 1941 ski trails were allowed on Whiteface Mountain. In 1947 they were added to Gore, South, and Pete Gay Mountains in Warren County. Saranac Lake made a land exchange in 1963 for refuse disposal. Piseco got land for the Piseco Airport in 1965 and in 1991.

Some of the suggested variations of the "forever wild" protection have gained widespread attention. The trade of lands in the Perkins Clearing area by the State and the International Paper Company to correct the "checkerboard" ownership was well-publicized and passed. The acquisition of the service buildings at the great camp at Sagamore was a well-won proposal. The State gained two hundred acres of wild forest lands and the historic buildings were saved.

Placing the decision for amending the "forever wild" provision of the New York State Constitution in the hands of the voters who own the Adirondack Forest Preserve lands is a good system. The protection provided to New York's great wilderness has held true for over one hundred years and, if the voter's continue to study the amendments and to make the wise choices, the Adirondacks will be here for generations to come.

FOREVER WILD

"Forever wild" has governed the use of the Adirondack Forest Preserve for over one hundred years. The citizens of New York State wisely included *in perpetuum* protection of the Adirondacks in the New

York State Constitution in 1894. "The lands of the state constituting the forest preserve shall be forever kept as wild forest lands" Article XIV, Section 1, constitutional provision has come to be known simply as the "forever wild" provision.

The "forever wild" interpretation of the protection of public lands in the Adirondacks has a history of compromise, adjustments, legal rulings, voter decisions, and misunderstandings. It has shouldered the blame and/or credit for most of the Adirondack decisions made in this century.

The Temporary Study Commission on the Future of the Adirondacks, appointed by Governor Nelson Rockefeller in 1968, wrestled with the "forever wild" designation in the late sixties and early seventies. They generated one hundred eighty-one recommendations which led to the creation of the Adirondack Park Agency. The creation of the APA led to the approval of the Adirondack Park State Land Master Plan by Governor Rockefeller to manage the publicly owned lands. It is the plan that guides our stewardship of the "forever wild" Adirondacks today.

It appears impossible for us, with our human frailties, to strictly adhere to a total, pure "forever wild" Adirondacks. Therefore, we have developed a plan for the use of the lands we own within the Adirondack Park. The plan classifies the some 2.8 million acres of state-owned land into nine designations. They range from wilderness to travel corridors. Each designation has its own definition describing the degree of deterrents disposed on the designated dominion. Wilderness is the most restrictive with primitive, canoe, and wild forest designations each a little less restrictive for human use.

Wilderness areas meet the pure definition of "forever wild." They are devoid of human traces; man is a visitor who does not remain and (hopefully) leaves nothing behind. Wilderness areas are left in their natural condition. They offer the greatest level of solitude or primitive recreation. Generally, the wilderness areas comprise over ten thousand acres of land offering the human creature a unique opportunity to commune with nature.

Fifteen wilderness areas have been designated within the Adirondack Park. They total slightly over a million acres of the six million acre park. Seven hundred fifty-five bodies of water and seven hundred miles of foot trails are included in this wilderness.

At last report, some non-conforming uses still remain in the Adirondack wilderness areas including ninety-four lean-tos, six miles of snowmobile trails, a fire tower, four state cabins, five horse barns, some telephone lines, and twelve miles of roads. Ideally, all non-conforming uses will cease.

The wilderness areas are spread throughout the Adirondack counties. Blue Ridge is located in the towns of Arietta, Lake Pleasant and Indian Lake. The Siamese Ponds wilderness area is located in the towns of Lake Pleasant, Wells, and Indian Lake in Hamilton County and in the towns of Johnsburg and Thurman in Warren County. It has the largest section of trailless wilderness in the state within its boundaries. Silver Lake area lies in the towns of Lake Pleasant, Benson, Wells and Arietta. Dix Mountain, Giant Mountain, High Peaks, Hoffman Notch, McKenzie Mountain, Pharaoh Lake, and Sentinel Range wilderness areas are in Essex County with some overlapping into adjacent counties. The High Peaks area is the largest with over 226,000 acres designated as wilderness. Five Ponds, Ha-de-ron-dah, Pepperbox, Pigeon Lake, and West Canada Lake areas are primarily in Herkimer County.

The "forever wild" Adirondacks of our predecessors are becoming a reality in our day. Our growing appreciation for the value of the wilderness experience guides our Adirondack decisions and moves us ever closer to the wilderness goal.

THE ADIRONDACK "NATIONAL PARK"

The United States of America can be proud of her national parks. They were identified and saved during a period of history when good people everywhere were realizing that some of our natural environment was worth saving and a benefit to the citizens of our nation. Over two hundred national parks and monuments are enjoyed by millions every year and have become a part of our national heritage. They are superior to crown jewels.

Have you ever visited the Adirondack National Park? You cannot! There has never been an Adirondack National Park and probably never will be. It was an idea whose time came and went; public outcry by those who love the Adirondacks ended any suggestion of national ownership of New York's Adirondack region.

A quarter of a century ago an Adirondack National Park was a possibility. The powerful Rockefeller family, brothers Laurance, chairman of the New York State Council of Parks and Outdoor Recreation, and New York Governor Nelson, recommended establishing a 1.72-million-acre national park in the heart of the Adirondack Forest Preserve. It required New York State to turn over some sixty million dollars worth of land to the federal government and private owners to relinquish some five million dollars worth. It would be the most impressive of the 32 major national outdoor parks at that time.

Those who supported the proposal promised extensive economic benefits to the region. Federal dollars would flow in and some 100 million people in the northeast would make use of the park. Great Adirondack acreage would be preserved for the people of America.

Opponents to the national park cited the loss of hunting lands; most national parks prohibit hunting. New regulations on logging and mining would supersede the "forever wild" provision. Some asked who paid for the two-year study which led to the surprise recommendation.

Others thought that the national park proposal was an insult to the abilities of the New York State Conservation Department and the people of the state to maintain the Adirondack State Park. The constitutional convention, coincidentally (or not so coincidentally) meeting in Albany, at the time, reinforced the state's commitment to the "forever wild" Adirondacks.

No one knew about the Adirondack Park proposal until it was released like a bomb in the summer of 1967. Legislators were not informed, the Adirondack Park Association knew nothing, the New York State Conservation Council was uninformed, and the general populous was devoid of even a rumor. It was a big secret and, once out in the open, was opposed by most New Yorkers. ˄

The study commission listed six reasons for creating a national park in the Adirondacks:

1. The Adirondacks are of national significance.
2. There was a need for a large national park for the 100 million in the northeast.
3. The Adirondack Park would not duplicate existing national parks.
4. Large state land ownership made the park feasible.
5. New York State needed help to purchase additional park lands.
6. National policies provide for better conservation and use.

Laurance Rockefeller, who was also serving as President Johnson's chairman of the Citizens Advisory Committee on Recreation and Natural Beauty, suggested that compromises could be worked out with lumbermen, hunters, landowners, and other concerned citizens. He also conceded that the bottom line was, because of the New York State Constitution, "If we are to have a national park in our state it will be brought about by the most democratic way of all—a direct vote of the people."

Assemblyman Glenn Harris asked for a clarification of the means used to establish a national park. Secretary of the Interior Stewart Udall had suggested that Congress had the power to create the national park in New York State without voter approval .

The national park proposal died from lack of support. Governor Rockefeller decided that he was "neither for or against." The Conservation Department made no recommendation but concluded that the proposed park would disorganize the timber industry, shut off hunting areas, upset the balance of nature, and change ownership of New York's water supply.

The Governor decided, instead, to appoint a temporary committee to study the future of the Adirondacks. And that is another story.

VII

Adirondack Geology

ADIRONDACK MOUNTAIN GEOLOGY

Adirondack guide and hotel keeper Paul Smith used to joke that the giant mountains around his hotel were just knolls when he moved there. It was done in jest, of course, but it had a ring of truth to it. Geological history of the Adirondacks indicated that they were grounded down to a plain at least twice during their long history. The "everlasting hills" may not be so everlasting.

Geology has been one of my hobbies since I spent some of my college days searching for rock samples in the Adirondacks with an outstanding science professor, Dr. June Lewis. She believed in learning by doing and taught science the way it should be taught. Introducing me to Adirondack geology was a major contributor to my lifelong love and understanding of the Adirondack region.

Geology is an ever-changing study. Theories explaining the formation of the Adirondacks have changed within my own lifetime. The old explanations have become obsolete.

For years it was believed that the Adirondacks were rebounding from the weight of the glacier. They are rising four times as fast as the Swiss Alps, about a mile every million years. The cause is unknown today. Rebounding is happening in other places where there never was a glacier. Some relate it to intense heat underneath the earth's crust. Someday we may have our own Adirondack volcano.

The Adirondacks are no longer believed to be part of the Appalachians. They are a unique circular dome made of rock that is much younger than previously believed.

The Adirondacks were possibly made of two continents which collided with one going underneath the other. The crash created mountains, valleys, and waters.

The University of the State of New York published Museum Bulletins in the early 1900's that are filled with geological history. They become an education in themselves with the amount of detail included within their covers. "The Geology of the Northern Adirondack Region" was published in 1905 and a full treatment of "The Adirondack Mountains" was published in 1917.

The old geology books are full of observations and advice. "It is

64

not at all surprising that people are frequently lost in the Adirondack woods. Persons not well acquainted with the Adirondack type of country should be careful not to wander away from well-defined trails or roads unless accompanied by a competent guide or some other person who really understands the region," is still good advice today.

"The excellent water of the Adirondacks deserves mention. Nearly all the streams which come down the mountain sides are clear, cold and pure," may not be as true today as it was at the beginning of the century. The days of drinking the water from any place in the Adirondacks is gone.

The Adirondacks were born of Mother Earth. The top came from inside the earth's crust. Studies show that molten lava found two six-mile exit canals back in geological history and flowed out creating a twelve thousand square mile canopy. The molten rock from inside formed a shield of hard anorthosite which forms a hard shell over the mountains. These facts strongly suggest that the Adirondack dome is of igneous origin with conduits that supplied the channels for the liquid magma to flow to the surface. A piece of this hard Adirondack anorthosite was transported to the Adirondack Museum at Blue Mountain Lake for those who want to "stand on the top of the Adirondacks." One geologist summed it up for us all with "the structure and origin of the Adirondack anorthosite has been the subject of geological controversy for decades."

There is still much to be learned about the unique geology of the Adirondack Mountain region. Possibly, William Miller hit on the reason more needs to be done in *Geology of the Lake Pleasant Quadrangle*, published in 1916. "The difficulties of doing detailed geological work in such a region, typically Adirondack in character, being rugged, densely wooded and sparsely settled, are impossible of appreciation by the uninitiated!"

THE WELLS OUTLIER

School children instinctively collect pretty stones and unique rocks and those who do it around the Hamlet of Wells are in for a rare treat. Wells, in the southern portion of the Adirondacks, enjoys some notoriety in the field of geology known only to those who have studied the land beneath their feet. Wells is a sedimentary island in the sea of the metamorphosed Adirondacks. It is unique and, because of its uniqueness, it has been the subject of study for many years.

The Wells Outlier was the subject of attention over one hundred years ago by Professor Ebenezer Emmons in his 1842 *Geology of the Second District*. In 1893 it was included in a study of the Mohawk Valley by Nelson Daton. Wells became the subject of a preliminary study of Hamilton County by J. F. Kemp, D. H. Newland, and B. J. Hill in 1898. Rudolf Ruedemann established the presence of ancient seas in his 1898 work on this area. New York State's *Geology of the Lake Pleasant Quadrangle* by William J. Miller, published in 1916, discusses the structure at length. In 1937, G. Marshall Kay verified the importance of the limestone deposits in Wells. And in July of 1957, Donald W. Fisher, New York State Paleontologist, published his detailed manuscript, *Mohawk Biostratigraphy of the Wells Outlier, Hamilton, County, New York*. The lands around Wells got a lot of attention.

The Wells Outlier, once the bottom of an ancient sea, is an ideal location for an Adirondack hamlet. Surrounded by the rolling lowland mountains, it provides the best in Adirondack beauty and security. Its floor is a gold mine of ancient fossils and unique geological formations. Students of the glacier will find splendid kames, small rolling hills left by glacial deposits, and erratics, large boulders left by the moving ice, balancing on the mountainside.

The fossil beds in Wells are endless with everything from Brachiopods to Trilobites. Most are in exposed beds and easily visible. Rockhounds will find Potsdam sandstone, Trenton limestone, Little Falls dolomite, Lowville limestone, and Canajoharie shale. Wells has a little bit of everything including the northern portions of the Mohawk Valley block "faulting."

There are many reasons why the scholars over the years have found the Wells Outlier worthy of study. A geological "outlier," to put it simply, is a unit of land which is different from that around it. The uniqueness of the Wells Outlier is caused by the presence of unmetamorphosed strata from one period of time surrounded by the metamorphosed Adirondack mountains from another period of formation. Why this happened is one of the Adirondack's greatest mysteries.

The preservation of the sedimentary rocks in Wells is partially attributed to the faulting which occurred back in history. The V-shaped valley was created by a major fault or shifting of the land mass on each side with a minor fault passing through Wells Village. The area contains a twenty-eight-mile fault along the East Branch of the Sacandaga, a six-mile fault running north-northeast, a fault through the village, and some other minor faults. From the geological standpoint, the dissection of this region by numerous faults is a feature of "principal interest."

Wells not only has its "faults" but it was once all wet. Geologist believe that the Wells Outlier was once covered by a Canadian sea or the ancient Grenville sea extending from Glens Falls across the Adirondacks.

Evidence also points to the existence of a glacial lake in the same region. An ice dam below the village held back the water in the river channel forming a lake three and a half miles long and two-thirds mile wide. The surface was at 1,020 feet at a time when the Adirondacks were several hundred feet lower. Glacial scratches have been found at the height of 2,200 feet in Wells. The ice was once over five hundred feet deep, placing Wells in the deep freeze.

Wells has an interesting geological history. There are many questions still to be answered. William J. Miller in his 1916 writings commented, "The difficulties of doing detailed geological work in such a region are impossible of appreciation by the uninitiated." Today, the uninitiated as well as the serious student of the out-of-doors appreciates the work done by scholars over the years. Slow down on your next trip through Wells, and turning your gaze to the surrounding lands and hills, imagine the unique geological history and the answers yet to come.

THAR'S GOLD IN THEM THAR HILLS

In my younger years I was told that the Kunjamuk Cave was once a gold mine, discovered by an ancient prospector searching the mountains of the remote Adirondacks for the mother lode. It made a good story, along with all of the other claims of great gold discoveries in the Adirondacks.

State Surveyor Verplanck Colvin called Benson the "gold mining district" in the 1880's. In the 1890's "gold fever" reached its greatest pitch in the Adirondacks. During this same period the Adirondacks became the subject of the Klondyke Experiment. By 1898 New York State recorded four thousand claims to gold and silver discoveries, mainly in the Adirondacks. Did anybody get rich? I think not; there was no recorded instance where the public received any financial return for its investment. The *Hamilton County History* (Aber, King) is filled with the stories of the attempts at gold mining in the Adirondacks.

Although gold has not made anyone rich in the Adirondacks, it is there. The stream and lake basins of the Adirondacks are filled with gravel and sand deposits. These have been formed by the erosive actions of water and ice on the local rocks. It is this process that gave rise to the gold fever. Traces of gold are usually found in such sands but the value is only a few cents at ton, hardly worth a mining operation.

In the early 1900's several tests were conducted on Adirondack gold. Prospectors claimed the gold to be worth from four to forty dollars per ton. Gold in Hadley was said to be yielding $7.50 per ton. Lewis County had some said to be almost four dollars per ton. When the claims were checked by impartial, reputable assayers, they ranged from a few cents up to less than three dollars per ton.

Man's greed sometimes blinds him to the truth. Investors were told by the promoters that the gold present in the Adirondacks could not be detected by ordinary chemical or assay methods because it existed in some peculiar state called "nascent," "atomic," or "volatile." They built plants to extract this special gold by secret methods. No record of a single ounce of gold from these mines can be found.

Some miners were fooled by other Adirondack minerals. Loose flakes of mica and mica-bearing rocks were shown to investors. Pyrite or "fool's gold" often appeared.

The old gold mining claims are available on microfiche at the New York State Library. Claims were sent to the Secretary of State for recording. Edward Berry sent one in as early as 1866.

> "I give you notice that on or about the 25th of August, 1866, I, the undersigned, residing in the Town of Wells, discovered and found a silver and gold mine and I claim discovery of the same. The discovery of the said mine was made on the farm where I now reside and joining lands contained in the survey: commencing at the Pumpkin Holer Rodad on the bank of the Sacondaga River and running down the river to the mouth' of East Stony Creek then up the creek to Smith and Co's Tannery: thence to Willis Lake: thence back to the Pumpkin Holer Road to the place of beginning."

Another example of a claim filed from the Town of Wells was a gold discovery on the Ostrander Creek. It was filed by Franklin J. Couch and Clark Satterlee in November of 1866. The gold was found where the bridge crossed the creek and the claim included a course of 100 chains up the creek on both sides. Apparently, they planned to pan the creek for the gold dust.

It is interesting to read the old gold mining claims but it is wise to avoid a case of "gold fever." Old gold mining claims were cancelled by the State Legislature in the 1940's. But, who knows, there may be a mountain of gold hiding deep in that Adirondack wilderness.

VIII

Adirondack Transportation

ADIRONDACK STAGE LINES

We often hear of the important part the stagecoach played in the romantic history of the old West, yet, we rarely place the same prominence on the stage lines in the Adirondacks. They were there. And they were important.

During the last half of the nineteenth century everything depended on the stagecoach in the Adirondacks. The early stage lines carried the people, the parcels, the mail, and the news to the remote settlements of New York's wilderness. The arrival and departure of the stagecoaches was a major event in the lives of the isolated settlers and visitors in the Adirondacks.

Some of the stagecoach lines in the Adirondacks ran on a regular schedule; some set their clocks with the comings and goings of the stagecoach. The drivers knew everyone on the route and were called upon to carry messages and to do errands. They brought medicine and gossip—two "necessities" for survival in the rural Adirondacks.

Adirondack stagecoach drivers were, of necessity, highly skilled. One error on a narrow, holey, bumpy, muddy, corduroy, wilderness road with its steep grades and sharp curves could cause a major tragedy. They remained cool and resourceful in times of danger and became hardened to fatigue and exposure. Some of their travel was in darkness. And yet, according to Adirondack historian Alfred Donaldson, "The Adirondack stagecoach drivers never had a fatal accident!"

The first regular stage lines connected three early hotels: Martins, Bakers, and Bartletts. The routes started from Elizabethtown, Keeseville, and Ausable Forks and crossed over to Franklin Falls, Bloomingdale, Paul Smiths, and the Saranacs. Others took a fork to Lake Placid and Keene Valley. When the railroad came to North Creek in 1871 the stages went into Raquette Lake country, Blue Mountain Lake and Long Lake. Settlements grew up on the stage lines at major forks and halfway points.

There was some famous drivers among the some two dozen best known. George Meserve drove baggage wagons during the Civil War for generals McClellan, Burnside, Hooker, and Grant. Beginning in 1878 he drove six-horse coach for Paul Smiths Hotel for twelve years.

He left to go to New Jersey to drive for Grover Cleveland.

Alexander Fitch O'Brien could drive a coach on the darkest night. He was the first to take a Concord Coach and Four over the Wilmington Notch Road. He was the last to drive a stage between Lake Placid and Saranac Lake.

Phil McManus was known for his sense of humor. One night he arrived late to face the wrath of those awaiting his arrival. He explained, "Mark Clough (a guide with big feet) asked me to bring him some leather for a new pair of shoes. I managed to bring him enough for one shoe tonight, but it slowed us down. I'll fetch the other tomorrow—so I'll probably be late again." The joke stayed on for years to explain every late stage.

"There comes the stage" can still be heard around the Wells Post Office at mail time. However, today's "stage" is a modern truck without horses. The reference to "stage" is a holdover from the days when George E. VanArnum operated a line from Northville to Lake Pleasant.

The early train lines from Gloversville terminated at Northville, the southern terminus of the Adirondacks. The stagecoaches took over from there. The *Hamilton County Press* reported in 1877 that the stage left Northville for Hope Centre, Wellstown, and Lake Pleasant on Tuesday and Friday at 8 A.M. The return trips were made on Wednesday and Saturday leaving Lake Pleasant at 3 A.M. Earlier, in the 1860's, a stage from Amsterdam to Northville took seven hours and made Northville the gateway to the Adirondacks.

Charlie Straight was the best-known driver on the route from Northville to Lake Pleasant. He was the most popular of the drivers who made the trip up the Hamilton Lake Road directly to Lake Pleasant or over the Gilmantown Road to Speculator. It was not until the Twentieth Century that the old log road up the Sacandaga River to Speculator was developed into a state road.

The stage line was an important link in getting the summer visitors to their destinations, and the hotels depended on these lines. The Northville-Lake Pleasant stage made a detour during the summer season taking supplies, visitors, and mail over the some twenty miles of dirt road to the Whitehouse, west of Wellstown. Stages loaded with deer during the hunting season were photographed at Northville and made into postcards. Women and children were able to join their fathers and husbands on Adirondack vacations. Thus, the development of the Adirondacks owes much to the penetration of its depths by the stagecoaches.

ADIRONDACK RAILROADS

Do you want to buy some stock in the Sacketts Harbor and Saratoga Railroad Company? The southern route will go through the Sacandaga River Valley, south of Piseco Lake, and through the Black River Valley to Lake Ontario. The northern route will skirt the Hudson River, cross over to the south end of Raquette Lake, and then follow the Moose River up to the Black River Valley. It should open up the Adirondacks and bring prosperity to the region. Don't buy it! Like so many of the Adirondack railroad proposals, the promoters promised more than they could deliver.

The Sacketts Harbor and Saratoga Railroad Company incorporated some hundred and forty years ago and received an option to buy 250,000 acres of state-owned land for five cents an acre. An association was formed and stock sold before a serious mistake was discovered in the association articles. The confidence and interest of the investors were lost and with only thirty miles of track laid down, the company reached a financial crisis.

A new company was organized called the Lake Ontario and Hudson Railroad Company and investors were sought across the ocean in England. The Civil War interrupted the process and it failed again.

Another company was formed called the Adirondack Estate and Railroad Company. Dr. Thomas Durant eventually took control and changed the name to The Adirondack Company. He had built the Union Pacific across our nation and knew something about railroads. He acquired one million Adirondack acres and made an agreement for no taxes for twenty years. He planned a railroad across the Adirondacks to the St. Lawrence. The route would leave Saratoga, go to North Creek, veer north of Long Lake, go through the valley of the Raquette River to the foot of Tupper Lake, and proceed over to the Grasse River and Ogdensburgh. He made it as far as North Creek in 1871 and that was it. His son, William West Durant sold the route to the Delaware and Hudson Railroad in 1889.

There were many other schemes for railroads in the Adirondacks, but few reached fruition. Most were designed to connect the waterways and faced the impossible task of laying rail through the wilderness. Summer rains made bogs of the supply roads. Winter froze the ground too hard to be graded. All drilling and blasting had to be done by hand. The distant work camps could not be reached by the six horse teams and most of the supplies and hay had to be toted on men's backs. And the black workers from Tennessee arrived in overalls and bare feet to suffer in the cold north country. It should be noted that the railroads that were completed owe their existence to the stamina of the black employees.

The Manheim and Salisbury Railroad, later the Mohawk and St. Lawrence Railroad and Navigation Company planned a railroad and canal through Herkimer County to the St. Lawrence via Raquette Lake in the 1830's. It was strictly a "paper" company.

About the same time, a railroad was planned from Ogdensburgh to Lake Champlain across the Adirondacks with a southern route to Fort Kent and a northern route to Plattsburgh. It was another failure, although the Northern railroad used part of the route in 1845 to connect Ogdensburgh to Malone.

An act to build a railroad from Port Kent to Boonville was passed in 1646. The route was to go through Franklin Falls, Saranac River and Lakes, and Raquette River to Long Lake. Nothing ever came of it.

The first successful Adirondack railroad from the north began at Plattsburgh. The Whitehall and Plattsburgh Railroad Company opened in 1868. A spur to Ausable Forks was added in 1674.

The first successful Adirondack railroad from the south was Durant's Adirondack Railroad Company, mentioned above, which ran sixty miles from Saratoga to North Creek. It opened in 1871.

The first railroad to enter well into the mountains was the Chateaugay Railroad in 1877. The route ran seventy miles from Plattsburgh to Saranac Lake. Later a ten mile spur was extended to Lake Placid. The ten mile trip ticket cost ten cents in 1893. The original purpose for this railroad was to take prisoners to Dannemora Prison and later to serve the mines at Lyon Mountain.

Another penetration into the mountains was named Hurd's Road after John Hurd, the lumberman who built it. The route extended from Moriah to Tupper Lake in 1889. It changed Tupper Lake from a cow pasture to a village. Later it became part of the New York and Ottawa Railroad. A million dollar bridge over the St. Lawrence River was added in 1898 which collapsed upon completion. The New York Central took the line over in 1906.

The most "Adirondack" of the railroads was the Adirondack and St. Lawrence Railroad Company which opened the same year the Adirondack Park was established, 1892. It was conceived by Dr. Seward

Webb to get to his Adirondack "camp." The New York Central refused to build it and the state refused a right-of-way so he bought property and built it himself. The route connected Malone to Lake Clear with an additional spur to Saranac Lake. Later Herkimer was connected. The New York Central bought it and added Old Forge to the route.

New York State's early dreams of an Adirondack region networked with railroads connecting big manufacturing and farming communities never became a reality. The wilderness proved, once again, that man alone does not control the destiny of the unsurpassed Adirondacks.

ADIRONDACKS AND THE AUTOMOBILE

Do you remember the first cars? How about the double cylinder, water cooled, eleven-horsepower Autocar or the Columbia Victoria electric car? Do you remember the two-person, $850 Ford with the tonneau (extra seat attachment) or the PierceArrow made in Buffalo? How many remember the Franklin made in Syracuse and the steam-engined Stanley Runabout? I don't! They were all made before my time; they were among the eighty-eight "carriages" on the American market in 1904.

One of the above automobiles and any one of the others could have been the first horseless carriage to enter the Adirondacks. Alfred Donaldson, Adirondack historian, recorded the first appearance of an automobile in his 1921 *History of the Adirondacks*. It was July of 1902 when Mr. and Mrs. Herbert Sackett honeymooned to the Lower Saranac Lake and Paul Smith's Hotel in their horseless carriage. It required traversing roads not made for autos. And, I imagine, it frightened a few horses and left some surprised Adirondackers in its wake.

Harold Hochschild in *Township 34* published the log of a 1905 trip to the Adirondacks in a 1905 Winton automobile. During the trip they broke a spring, took everything out of the car to make the hills, and sometimes backed the car up the hills to keep the gasoline fed to the motor, a common practice in the early years of gravity fed gas tanks. They also had five flat tires on the trip, another common problem in early auto travel.

Adirondack historians, Stella King and Ted Aber, made note of other autos in the Adirondacks. They found that a small auto carrying two men drove through Hope on Route 30 in the summer of 1903. By

1905 an auto was occasionally seen on the main road through the village of Wells.

The commercial use of autos entered the scene with many of the settlers joining the profession of chauffeuring. John Ostrander and Ed Call of Lake Pleasant attempted an unsuccessful auto stage line in 1907. Narrow, undeveloped roads put them out of business.

Adirondack roads were rough, narrow, rocky, and rutty. They were not made for the new-fangled automobiles. William Philips put in a claim for "breaking of a automobile" on the rough, unfinished, Lewey Lake road in January of 1909.

Adirondack journalist, Oliver Wesley Whitman, recorded the first automobile ascending West Hill near Wells in 1911. In November of 1912 he had to pull an automobile to the top of West Hill with his horses. By 1913 his hunting and fishing parties were coming to the Adirondacks by automobile from Schenectady and Gloversville.

The automobile brought other problems to the Adirondackers. Dr. Joseph Head got his automobile stuck in a ditch in November of 1913. On March 23, 1915 he was run over by an automobile.

Apparently the automobiles were speeding on the Adirondack roads. Indian Lake set a speed limit of ten miles per hour on August 24, 1912 and, with some protesting, raised it to twenty miles per hour on September 9th. The same year the Town of Lake Pleasant set a town speed limit of thirty miles per hour.

Steamboats and railroads had made some encroachments into the Adirondacks in the 1800's and were doing well. The intrusion of the automobiles into Adirondack transportation had a disastrous affect on these existing forms of transportation and it was not long before they were forced to go out of business. Blacksmiths made career changes into boat building or mechanics.

Frank Leslie's *Popular Monthly Magazine* had predicted in 1904 that "the automobile will become an indispensable adjunct to modern civilization." They were right. The Adirondacks were changed forever with the advent of the automobile. Vacation habits changed. Inaccessible places became accessible. Exclusive places became less and less exclusive. And the Adirondack Park became a park with new roads, campsites, and trails. Thus, the automobile in the Adirondacks created a people's park and made the Adirondacks what they are today.

IX

Adirondack Waters

ADIRONDACK DAMS

What do you say we go up to the "Whitehouse Reservoir" near Wells to catch some fish this weekend? Can't be done; there is no Whitehouse Reservoir, although it was planned in 1912. The Whitehouse dam and several others were on the Adirondack drawing board over the years, never to be realized. Economics, legal restrictions, and outright opposition have been a part of Adirondack dam building for the last century.

The 1912 Report of the Conservation Commission proposed two dams on the West Branch of the Sacandaga River. The first dam was to be erected between Piseco Lake and the Whitehouse. The second dam was proposed for a Black Bridge location. Power houses were scheduled for Whitehouse and Black Bridge with power tunnels leading to each. Adirondack waterways are tempting sources of power and water supply.

The twelve major Adirondack counties have their share of dams. Official statistics record 945 dams of varying sizes with 378 of significant size. There are dams on the Sacandaga, Indian Lake, Cranberry Lake, Lake Placid, Goodnow Flow, Pharaoh Lake, Eagle Lake, Lake George outlet, Lake Durant, Lake Adirondack, Harrisburg Lake, Brant Lake, Stillwater and others. Man may have built more dams in the Adirondacks than the busy beavers.

The Association for the Protection of the Adirondacks was organized in 1901 to fight lumbering proposals around Raquette Lake by the State Fish, Game and Forest Commission. They planned to cut thousands of acres of virgin Adirondack timber. After this logging fight the association turned their attention to dams and successfully battled against dams on Higley Mountain, Panther Mountain, Salmon River, Lake Luzerne, and Gooley Mountain.

The Gooley Dam was in the news in the sixties. The dam was proposed on the Hudson just below the Indian River connection. The 16,000 acres of the resulting impounded waters would have covered the village of Newcomb, all of Lake Harris, and some of the D&H railroad and Huntington Wildlife Forest almost to Long Lake. The idea died and a State Study Commission recommended in June of 1969 that no more reservoirs should be planned within the confines of the Adirondack Forest Preserve.

The Adirondack dams were proposed for many reasons. Drinking water and canal uses compose the highest priority reasons. Flood control and power are the major purposes for many of the dams including Conklinville on the Sacandaga. Others were dammed to maintain water levels. The fish hatching beds on Adirondack lakes, such as Lewey Lake in Hamilton County, were reason enough to build a dam during the dam-building years.

The Adirondacks would be a different place without the dams. Although it is virtually impossible to propose and build any new dams today, we appreciate those constructed by our forefathers. Adirondack users have found recreational opportunities, second-home locations, and income production associated with the dammed waters of the Adirondacks. And in a future world, these impounded waters of the Adirondacks will be one of our most precious possessions.

THE SACANDAGA RIVER STORY

The Adirondack's Sacandaga River deserves more attention than it receives; its triple branches reach into more Adirondack country than is expected or known by most. The West Branch comes out of Piseco Lake Country. It reaches into Good Luck Lake and Silver Lake waters. The East Branch comes off of Gore Mountain and collects the waters of the Siamese Pond Wilderness area. The main branch holds the waters of Sacandaga Lake and Lake Pleasant on their journey to Wells and to the Great Sacandaga Lake.

The Sacandaga River lacks the designation of a watershed; this important Hudson River tributary is lumped in with the Upper Hudson River Drainage Basin. Adirondack surveyor Verplanck Colvin predicted before the turn of the century that the waters of the Adirondacks, including the Sacandaga, would be needed downstate. He was a true prophet; the Hudson River Basin Study of today calls for the use of the Adirondack waters for the cities to the south.

The Sacandaga is one of the most interesting rivers in New York State because of its anomalous course. It moves eastward across the Adirondacks instead of the normal southward; its circuitous route travels from the West Branch about eighty-eight miles before it joins the

Hudson at Luzerne, some thirty miles away. From Sugarloaf Mountain it flows southwestward, westward, northward, and then eastward to Whitehouse for a distance of twenty-eight miles and is then only four miles from its beginning. The abnormal sharp turn northeastward of the main branch at Northville was caused by the glacier; the original route continued southward to the Mohawk River. Another interesting occurence involves Fawn Lake and Sacandaga Lake. Less than a half mile apart they drain in opposite directions. Fawn Lake drains into Piseco Lake while the Sacandaga drains through Lake Pleasant. The two waters meet below Wells at the Forks.

Settlements grew up along the banks of the Sacandaga. Tanning and logging made use of its waters. Grist mills and saw mills used the power of the moving waters. Many of us are here today because the Sacandaga attracted our ancestors.

The waters of the Sacandaga River sired two great lakes. A dam at Wells, erected in 1925, created the 285-acre Lake Algonquin. The lake provides water recreation and power for the residents and visitors to this picturesque Adirondack hamlet.

The Wells dam was the site of a tragedy on January 1, 1949 when the dam went out taking the Whitman family home down the raging Sacandaga. The William Fremont family got out before the house broke up. Most of our family heirlooms were lost in the flood. The loss of the lake reduced the Sacandaga, once again, to the original river bed.

The citizens of Wells wanted the lake back and after a vote of 116 to 43 they approved $30,000 for dam reconstruction in July of 1949. The reconstructed dam was planned by town engineer Morrell Vrooman of Gloversville. C. A. Collins built a concrete replacement for $21,610. In 1959 a new modern dam was constructed for $190,000 to hold back the Sacandaga waters. In recent years the waters have been harnessed for electrical power.

The second great lake on the Sacandaga River is the Great Sacandaga Lake. Originally called a reservoir, it creates power and prevents flooding on the Hudson River's southerly flow. It has become one of New York's great recreational lakes. Before the dam was constructed at Conklinville, the Sacandaga River made its way through the Adirondacks to the Hudson. Over forty square miles were flooded causing the removal of trees, hamlets, and cemeteries. Sacandaga Park, the "Coney Island of the North," declined after the loss of the Sacandaga River which flowed through its bounds and provided recreation for thousands.

The late Adirondack folk singer, Pete Craig of Wells, paid tribute to the Sacandaga River in a song written a half century ago. It tells of the coming of the Indians and the white man, the water power, the logging, and the flooding. He concludes:

> This old river has watched many men come and go
> And with all that has happened still it will flow,
> Rough raging wildness or calm as can be,
> It will run down the valley until it reaches the sea.

THE SACANDAGA DAM

There was talk of damming the Adirondacks. Building dams would create vast new fishing waters, control flooding, and provide needed power. It was 1911. Farmers in the Sacandaga River country were hired to remove stone from the riverbed. Measurements were being taken to determine the amount of power that could be gained by a dam at Conklinville. Preliminary studies in 1907 had raised the possibility of a dam on the Sacandaga. A dam had been suggested by state surveyor Verplanck Colvin during the past century.

The dam on the Sacandaga was completed in 1930. It was not without controversy; there were those who had good reasons for opposing the flooding of the Sacandaga Fly (Vlaie). Sportsman mourned the loss of their hunting and fishing grounds. It was a paradise. From the days of Sir William Johnson the vlaie had supplied an abundance of fish and game for their tables. The nine streams and endless marshes of the Sacandaga Vlaie teemed with northern pike, pickerel, walleye pike, bass, and bullheads. Game birds and animals thrived in the Sacandaga wooded environment. There were very few places where you could find deer, partridge, fox, and raccoons so close to a population center. Many were opposed to the loss of such a lush wilderness area in the Adirondack foothills.

Others called the new lake created by the dam on the Sacandaga, "Desolation." My grandmother bemoaned the loss of my great-grand-parent's home in Osborn Bridge. She recalled the disturbing of graves in twenty-two cemeteries which had to be moved to make way for the impending waters. She remembered the thousands of stumps near Sacandaga Park where the giant trees were removed. She found no value in the new lake created by the dam.

The name "Sacondaga" (original spelling) came from the Dutch and meant low, swampy, or drowned lands. It was a natural area in which to create the large forty-two square mile Great Sacandaga Lake. Unfortunately, it covered the villages of Osborn Bridge, Munsonville, Day, and West Day, and parts of Edinburg and eight other villages. It covered the FJ&G railroad tracks, parts of Sacandaga Park and uncounted roads and bridges. A price beyond dollars was paid for the twelve million dollar dam.

Flooding in downstate areas was the primary reason for damming up the Sacandaga. Flooding down the Hudson was severe in 1913 and 1922. Residential areas were flooded and epidemics erupted. Downtown Albany was flooded. A steady source of power was needed by industries along the Hudson and the Hudson River Regulating District, established by the 1922 state legislature, was empowered to deliver. The cost of the dam was paid by the communities and commercial enterprises which benefited from the lake.

The fluctuating shoreline caused by the demand for down river water and flood control was a part of our childhood although we never questioned its occurrence. All we knew was that the water got further and further from our beach toward the end of the summer and the beach became muddier and muddier. We knew that in the spring the fish would be feeding well up into the flooded shorelines. We skated when the ice was thick and recorded the date of the ice going out each year. We helped Floyd Arnold wire brush and repair his wide wooden row boats each year for rental at his boat livery. We quickly learned to swim by jumping off the boat dock; no one wanted to step on the muddy flats under the water. We bought Northville soda pop at the boat livery store for a nickel earned by picking up empty pop bottles along the highway. We picked mint and dug horseradish along the exposed Sacandaga mud flats. This Great Sacandaga combined with the Adirondack wilderness was a great place to grow up and we took it for granted.

Other dams have been proposed in the Adirondacks. Dams were built on many of the lakes to raise their levels and to provide power. Dams were built on rivers and streams for power and to create fishing ponds. Dams proposed on Panther Mountain, Higley Mountain, and Gooley on the Upper Hudson were opposed by citizens of the state and never built. Others have been suggested on most of the waters of the lower Adirondacks. A lot of water has gone over the dam since the early studies to dam the Sacandaga, yet it now appears that the days of building major dams on Adirondack waters are over.

X

Adirondack Hiking and Camping

"FREE" ADIRONDACK ENTERTAINMENT

People pay big bucks to find enjoyment and stress-relief at man-made amusements; it is a short-lived remedy. The great out-of-doors is free and it can bring a lifetime of enjoyment to those who discover its offerings. And there is no better out-of-doors than the vast Adirondack Mountains of New York State.

The Adirondacks offer the obvious, i.e., hiking, swimming, camping, hunting, and fishing. And they offer the not-so-obvious that appeals to young and old when they take the time to penetrate the depths of the Great Wilderness.

I have found, during my lifetime, that I have enjoyed a number of Adirondack activities and they continue to bring happiness when they are relived or resurrected from my aging memory bank. They may bring enjoyment to you.

I remember:

Taking a ride on an old inner tube on the West Bank of the Sacandaga River on a sizzling summer day.

Sitting on the cliff overlooking Jimmy Creek falls while enjoying a good book.

Searching for minerals in the bottom of Bennett Lake from a leaky wooden boat.

Squeezing an overnight stay in an Adirondack lean-to into a busy schedule.

Catching frogs, crayfish, and minnows in a cool mountain stream.

Sliding on the smooth rock ledges in the white waters of a rushing mountain creek.

Enjoying the view from some of the lesser mountain peaks.

Hiking in the evening to the picturesque Auger Falls.

Sitting in a boat on an Adirondack lake letting the drama of night fall around me.

Getting up early and watching the heavy fog lift spookily off a mountain lake from the shore or from a boat.

Spending time camping with friends and family in an Adirondack setting.

Telling tales and watching skits around an Adirondack campfire.

Lying in an Adirondack field watching the fireflies flicker on and off.

Stretching out on an Adirondack hillside to face a Heaven full of stars.

Spending a lazy summer afternoon paddling and pulling a guide-boat through the meandering West Branch of the Sacandaga River.

Riding through the Adirondack back country roads on a hot summer night in a convertible.

Sitting on top of Hadley Mountain searching for signs of man in the green ocean of forest below.

Counting the waters from the top of Snowy Mountain.

Enjoying the fellowship and relaxation in a State campsite.

Discovering one of Colvin's surveying bolts on a remote mountaintop.

Finding a hillside covered with pink lady slippers.

Bushwhacking through the thick Adirondack forest growth where no man walked before.

Catching a glimpse of Adirondack wildlife while touring, hiking, and/or camping.

Exploring Adirondac, Tomantown, Griffin, Tirrell Pond Settlement, Oregon, and other "ghost towns" of the days gone by.

Parking the car and walking through the Adirondack Hamlets, stopping to shop, or talk, or eat where time stands still.

Discovering an Adirondack Great Camp and getting a chance to walk through.

Visiting a log job in Tennantville and spending time at a lumber mill.

Finding an unexpected supply of gourmet Adirondack mushrooms.

Listening to the early morning sounds of the birds claiming their territories or calling friends.

Waking up in the night to the chilling sound of the loon or owls or coyotes.

Snowshoeing the quiet winter woods.

Being alone in the stillness of the Adirondack forest where the mind clears and the body is fine-tuned!

The list goes on; there is something for everyone in the Adirondacks. The health-giving wilderness is more than a haven for mosquitoes and wild beasts; it is a place where humankind can find cost-free entertainment and freedom from stress.

THE NORTHVILLE-LAKE PLACID TRAIL

How would you like to take a hundred thirty-three mile hike in the woods? It is possible in New York State. The premier trail of the Adirondacks is the Northville to Lake Placid Trail. Created by the Adirondack Mountain Club in 1922, its seventy-year history is filled with triumphs and tragedies. The Northville-Lake Placid Trail has been mastered by some and remains a mystery to others.

The Northville-Lake Placid Trail's southern starting point is at the west end of the Northville bridge. It was selected in the early years because the railroad terminus was at that point. An historic marker indicates the site of the depot near the bridge. The train dropped the hikers at that end, the hikers walked the trail, and then caught another train at Lake Placid, the northern end. Later, bus service (F.J.&G.) took the hikers to Northville and, although it ceased for many years, bus service is once again available from Gloversville to Northville.

Those who drive to the Adirondack's longest trail usually pick up the trail at Benson, about ten miles up the road from the bridge. It eliminates the hike along Route 30 from Northville to Benson.

Many believe that once they start they must hike the entire one hundred thirty-three miles. Not true. The Northville-Lake Placid Trail is intersected by main roads at four points. It is a simple matter to leave the trail at Whitehouse near Wells, Route 8 at Piseco, Route 30 near Blue Mountain Lake, or Route 28N near Long Lake. Branch trails provide additional choices to terminate a hike. The Northville-Lake Placid Trail offers opportunities for day hikes, overnight hikes, or longer sojourns in the wilderness.

Each section of the Trail has something to offer. Taking a day hike in and out the Benson end of the Trail can be enjoyable. Easy hiking, a rustic bridge, a nearby stream, and the mixture of plants, trees, birds, and animals combine to provide a positive outdoor experience.

A different kind of experience can be gained by walking up the trail from Whitehouse to Piseco. A side trip to the Big Eddy on the West Branch of the Sacandaga is an option. The Hamilton Stream lean-to is about two miles up the trail and the walking is easy. Roadways once passed through this area of the Adirondacks and the stone fences, apple trees, and lilac bushes of the early settlers can be seen. Quiet hikers may observe some of the resident animals.

Parking at the trailhead near Blue Mountain Lake and hiking in to

Tirrell Pond takes the hiker back in history. Tirrell was once a thriving community; Father Michael Olivetti of Whitehall purchased 12,500 acres of Township 19 for $4,000 in 1851 and created a settlement for Irish immigrants from Ticonderoga. The immigrants were not always accepted by the communities and the good priest tried to help them to form their own. Life is tough in the mountains and the Tirrell Pond community did not survive. There are other stories of settlements at Tirrell Pond of mystery and disease that are still told today. It is hard to imagine a community situated where today you see a quiet pond with its sandy beaches surrounded by wilderness. Beyond the history, there are also cliffs and caves for exploring on the far side of the pond, another attraction for the hiker of today.

Guidebooks have been written for those who plan to hike the Northville-Lake Placid Trail. They provide the details for each section of the Trail and are helpful in making choices for hikes. The Adirondack Mountain Club printed the first guidebook in 1934 and has revised and reprinted it several times over the years.

The Northville-Lake Placid Trail is marked with blue trail markers. There is no reason to get lost hiking the trail if the hiker *stays on the trail* and *makes good decisions*. Those who experience difficulties choose to leave the main trail or are careless in following the blue markers.

The trail has enough lean-tos to provide sleeping quarters each night. Carrying a small tarp or tent helps if the lean-to is filled up. The rule is that a lean-to is made to be shared as long as there is room. There is a long tradition of coed sleeping in the Adirondack lean-tos.

It can be a challenge to those who choose to cover the distance in a set time. It can be a joy to those who choose to select one section at a time. It brings thousands to the Adirondack mountains and lakes each year and, with proper care, will continue to do so for years to come.

THE ADIRONDACK FORTY-SIXERS

There are those who climb the high peaks of the Adirondacks and count the climbs. They obtain the title of "Adirondack Forty-Sixer" once they reach the summits of the forty-six highest mountains in the Adirondacks. It is a challenge and an accomplishment for many. The list of the conquerors of the highest peaks includes those who did it in their parents' packbaskets and those who completed the challenge in their senior years.

Some get carried away with the obsession to set a forty-six record. Twenty years ago a thirty-year-old hiker attempted to complete the forty-six peaks in five days. He did not make it. He was carried off the south face of Mt. Marcy. He had made it to just below the summit where he collapsed and died.

Two months after this unfortunate death, two others attempted the same feat. A couple of seventeen-year-old counselors from Camp Pok-O-Moonshine completed the ascent of the forty-six Adirondack high peaks in less than seven days. They wanted to beat the record of eleven days set in 1962 and the nine-day record set in 1969. The total ascent is some 60,000 feet, (quite a feat!). It requires the climbing of between four and nine mountains each of the seven days.

In 1925 the Forty-Sixers were born. Three hikers, Robert and George Marshall, and Adirondack guide, Herbert Clark, completed the climb of forty-six Adirondack peaks and began a quest that was multiplied into the present generation.

The Adirondack Mountain Club published Robert Marshall's account of the climbs of forty-two peaks in 1922. Four others were added a couple years later. In 1928 Russell M. L. Carson added to the Adirondack high peak interest with his book, *Peaks and People of the Adirondacks*.

Some of the mountain clubs and Boy Scouts took up the high peak hike but little interest was generated in climbing the Adirondack High Peaks in those early days. One exception was the young people of the Grace Methodist Church in Troy. Their minister, the Reverend Ernest R. Ryder, had lived in the Adirondacks and loved to climb. He not only encouraged his young people to climb the Adirondacks but was known to hold his Sunday worship service on top of the mountains. He finished the forty-six peaks on September 13, 1936 and six months later the Forty-Sixers were organized. The Grace Methodist Church then spawned the first Forty-Sixers.

The Forty-Sixers had the purpose of "bringing together mountain enthusiasts and their friends who have climbed the Adirondacks so that they may share experiences and cooperate with the spirit of the 'forever wild' provision of the Constitution." Their aim is to climb the forty-six major peaks of the Adirondack Mountains. In the beginning the climbers were to complete at least one mountain per year. By 1946, forty-six Forty-Sixers had recorded their climbs.

A word should be said about the forty-six peaks for those who want to complete the climb. Originally the peaks were all listed in the four thousand feet or more range. They are still referred to, in many cases, as the forty-six peaks over four thousand feet. New and more accurate methods of measuring peaks has taken four mountains off the over four thousand feet list and changed the altitude of all but five others. Nye, Blakes Peak, Cliff, and Couchsachraga are in the 3,800 to 3,900-feet range. Marcy, Nippletop, Redfield, Lower Wolf Jaw, and Seymour retain their original heights.

There are many who choose to be unrecorded Adirondack High Peak climbers. There are those who make the effort to climb and record their success in the special containers to become "Forty-Sixers." I think that I will be content to just climb Cathead forty-six times.

THE FORKS

"Let's go up to 'The Forks' to the dance," was heard throughout Adirondack country during the first half of this century. "The Forks" refers to the Sacandaga Campsite where the Sacandaga River branches come together near Wells. Old newspaper clippings called it the Wells Campsite. Whatever it was called, it was the first public campsite in the state on Forest Preserve lands.

"The Forks" was developed in 1920 as a place for the people who owned the Adirondack Preserve to tent or picnic in natural surroundings. In the words of the Forest Commission, "It is difficult to estimate the great good that will be accomplished by a consistent development of such a policy (overnight camping facilities) for making more available the recreational facilities of our Adirondack Park." A 1921 report indicated that the campsites "have more than paid for themselves in the prevention of forest fires." A 1930 ruling somewhat "legalized" the campsites on Forest Preserve "forever wild" lands. Other sites were developed and today "The Forks" has been followed by some four dozen other state campgrounds in the Adirondacks.

By 1923 over 100,000 people had camped on state campsites. The "most popular" camping area was the Sacandaga Campsite where over 1,500 people had stopped during one day in July. In 1937 the county gave some additional land to the campsite. The popularity continued and in July of 1949 it was reported to the press that "The Forks" was turning away applicants. Forest Ranger Claude Simons announced that seventy-five new tent sites were being prepared across the river making it the largest campsite in the state at that time.

In the early days the Wells Campsite had its own variety store and dance hall. The newspaper ads simply stated "DANCING - Every Saturday Nite - GIRARDS - At 'The Forks.' " Everyone knew where it was. The city girls came up and danced with the boys from the mountains and the girls from the mountains danced with the city boys. Friendships were developed and weddings followed so that today many can trace their family beginnings back to "The Forks."

The live music at "The Forks" attracted both summer residents and residents from the surrounding communities. It was not unusual to have a full house on Saturday night. During the square dances the entire building, sitting on blocks, would bounce up and down to the beat of the music.

The Northville churches held their annual picnics at "The Forks." The heydays of the Sacandaga Park were over and the Wells Campsite was the nearest picnic grounds. Carloads would leave from the church and a day of swimming and picnicking in the natural surroundings was enjoyed by young and old. Sometimes we would stop at Howlands Mobil gas station and store, next to the Wankena Campgrounds in Hope, and get a treat.

The beach at "The Forks" would not compare with some of today's highly-developed beaches but in the early days, it was the best. The sand stretched along the Sacandaga River and bathers could sit under the trees or out in the sun. A small dam holds back the Sacandaga waters creating a sizeable swimming hole. We often accepted the challenge to swim to the opposite bank which was frowned upon by the state lifeguard.

The dam provided another challenge. Those who dared ventured out along the dam and sat under the cascading waters. It was a pretty sight to sit behind the small waterfall and observe the sun glistening on the other side of the waters.

Scout troops in the surrounding counties made good use of the campsite for camporees. The developed facilities along with the trails and river made "The Forks" an ideal spot for outdoor experiences. Our troop outings at "The Forks" were always well-attended.

There are bigger campsites in the Adirondack Forest Preserve today and those with fancy facilities and beaches but none will hold the memories we have of "The Forks." The thousands who enjoyed the campsite on the Sacandaga over the years, and those who still choose it today, can't help but smile when they hear, "Let's go up to The Forks!"

LOST IN THE ADIRONDACKS

Stories of those lost in the Adirondack Wilderness have been with us since 106-year-old, Abenaki Indian guide Sabael Benedict walked into the Adirondacks and disappeared in 1855. It still happens in the 1990's. Hikers, campers, scouts, hunters, and fishermen join the ranks of those who enter the Adirondack forest and fail to find their way out. Some are found and some are not.

Getting lost in the Adirondacks has one common thread; a series of poor choices. Answer the questions: Should I hike alone or with someone? Should I take a map and compass or rely on instinct? Should I stay on the marked trails or bushwhack? Should I drink the Adirondack waters or take precautions? Should I run ahead or drag behind the group or stay together? Should I start out late in the day or wait until tomorrow? Should I prepare for an unseasonable storm or take my chances?

We know the answers, yet, there are those, young and old, experienced and inexperienced who still choose the wrong answers. It could happen to any of us if we are not careful. We read about it in the papers and pay the costs of high priced searches. And some end in tragedy.

The Adirondack Forest Preserve, the land which belongs to you and I, encompasses some 2.7 million acres of the Adirondack Park. That calculates into almost 118 billion square feet. It's a lot of land in which to lose yourself!

The Adirondack Forest Preserve is a vast mixture of forests, waters and mountains. In some locations the trees form an endless maze of impenetrable foliage. Once lost in a canopy of forest branches it is impossible to see one from the air or ground.

Water can be a friend or foe. Those weighted down with heavy hunting or winter clothes have lost their lives on an Adirondack lake or pond. Overloaded boats tip easily and the cold, icy water claims the contents. Unseen water hiding in an Adirondack bog has claimed those who try to cross, drop through the brittle cover, and therefore are preserved forever in the oxygenless deep.

Fishing alone on a slippery, rock-filled Adirondack stream has cruelly claimed those who stumble and, knocked unconscious, drown in a foot of water. Georgia, the resident ghost of the Benson wilderness, was swallowed up in an Adirondack swamp in 1941.

Climbing an Adirondack mountain can be an exhilarating experience or an inutile tragedy. Falling and breaking a bone is not uncommon and somewhat expected. Getting caught in an unseasonable snowstorm is also not uncommon but the least expected by the uninitiated. Blinding snows and temperature drops have claimed their share of Adirondack hikers.

Getting lost is always preceded by an innocent activity. Two girls dropped off on a log road after a party, a young child straying away from the group picnic, a solitary afternoon walk in a well-known hiking area, a late season hike up a favorite mountain, a lifelong dream to hike the Northville-Lake Placid trail, are samples of some "lost in the Adirondacks" stories. None suspected the tragedy in store for them. None were prepared for the many moods of the Adirondacks. Some of those moods are tragic and those who enter the mountains should be aware.

Four circumstances are common to those found lost in the Adirondacks. They are usually walking in circles, cold, wet, and hungry. Some say we have one leg shorter than the other, hence, we walk in a circular pattern when lost. There are other theories to explain this pattern but, in any sense, take a compass and make certain you walk in a straight line. Without a compass, repeatedly sight a distant tree and walk to it.

The other factors need to be considered ahead of time. Carry warm clothing and matches, take raingear or at least a piece of plastic sheeting, and put some survival food in your pockets. These simple acts can turn a potential tragedy into a happy ending.

The old guides had their rules in the woods and they stuck to them. Their clients had to listen to them or the guide would go home. They, in this way, survived a lifetime of dealing with the wilderness without tragedy. The wilderness can also be yours if you set your rules and stick to them. Make good decisions and you will find a splendid wilderness, right on our doorstep, of peace, beauty, and never-ending pleasure.

XI

Adirondack Ghost Settlements

Foxlair burning .

GRIFFIN—LOST ADIRONDACK HAMLET

Hidden beneath the climax maples and giant pines of the Adirondack hillsides is the story of once-thriving homesteads and hamlets. One such hamlet, Griffin, was a major nineteenth century center of the tanning and lumbering industries on the East Branch of the Sacandaga River. It grew from the Adirondack wilderness, reached a peak of success, and returned from whence it came all within a quarter of a century.

The combination of a deer herd and hemlock trees spelled "profit" to American enterprise. Investing in a tannery was a lucrative venture in the days of the early Adirondacks. Tanneries sprang up wherever a good supply of hemlock trees was located. The tannic acid from the hemlock bark was a major ingredient in the tanning of hides. Griffin on Route 8, not too far beyond today's hamlet of Wells, offered what was perceived as an endless supply of hemlock trees.

A road from Wells led to Griffin in 1838 where some early settlers cleared their farms and where Charles Martin had erected a saw mill. In 1872, Catlin and Hunt moved in and built a mill for the "extraction of the tanning liquor from the hemlock bark." Thus began the thriving settlement along the Sacandaga.

Catlin and Hunt built a huge barn for their twenty teams of horses. They constructed a hotel and a boarding house, an office and a mill. They called the settlement Extract since their purpose was to gather the extract from the trees, take it by teams of horses to Amsterdam or Fonda, and ship it from there to commercial tanneries. They continued into the 1880's when the name was changed to Moons Mills. Jim Moon now owned and operated a large sawmill business on the site.

About this same time Stephen Griffing started a lumbering operation. He built a blacksmith shop, a large supply store, and a headquarters building. In 1877 he was selling hemlock bark to tanneries and built two tanneries of his own. The name then became Griffin, dropping the "g" from his name.

Early in the 1880's Rice, Emery and Co. took over the Griffing tannery business and made it one of the two largest in New York State. They began to ship in hides from all over the world for tanning at Griffin where the hemlock bark was plentiful. Thus the remote Adirondack settlement at Griffin became a major center of the tanning industry.

Lumbering and tannery workers were moving in all the time. The community was growing. Businesses, tannery houses, stores, hotels, and a saloon sprang up. A schoolhouse was built. The stage made a stop in Griffin on the way to North Creek. The telegraph was connected. The Morgan Lumber Co., later the International Paper Co., moved in and bought some of the Griffin interests. They built a large barn and a boarding house which still stands along Route 8 at Griffin.

The "boom" ended. The tannery business ceased in the 1890's because of the diminishing supply of hemlock bark and changes in the tanning process. H. J. Girard bought some of the Morgan Lumber Company holdings and operated a hotel and sugar bush for many years.

The hamlet where three hundred permanent residents made their homes, where two hundred lumberjacks spent Saturday nights, where bands from Northville came to perform, where a dancing bear entertained along the streets, where residents skated on the frozen river, and where proud and strong men from the woods and tanneries engaged in boxing matches, came to an end. The lumber from the houses was taken to the growing community of Wells for new homes and barns. Some was left to rot; today the stone foundations can be found among the trees in Griffin. Griffin returned to the Adirondack wilderness leaving behind the history of a once-thriving community.

THE HUDNUT ESTATE—ADIRONDACK LUXURY

For years motorists passed a sign on Route 8 between Wells and Weavertown in Hamilton County which said "FOX LAIR, POLICE ATHLETIC LEAGUE." Fox Lair is no more. Once the wealthy estate of the Hudnut cosmetic clan and later a boys camp operated by the Police Athletic League of New York City, it has returned to the Adirondack wilderness.

The story of the Hudnut Estate begins with Richard, son of New York City druggist, Alexander Hudnut. Richard joined his father's business and experimented with perfumes, developing the first Queen Anne Cologne. Thus, Fox Lair owes its existence to a perfume.

Richard married the wealthy Evelyn Beals and came to the Adirondacks in 1900. He purchased 1,200 acres in a valley on the East Branch of the Sacandaga River near Bakers Mills where he chose to build his baronial mansion. He hired a noted architect, as many of the early Adirondack "camp" builders did, and constructed a manor house, sports house, garage, stable, servants building, farm buildings, superintendents house, and a golf course. He repaired and built a better road to Bakers Mills. All this in the Adirondack wilderness.

The manor house, standing on a knoll overlooking the river, was a showplace. The living room alone was 50' x 50' long with a stone foundation built on solid rock. Richard purchased made-to-order furniture from France and bought French antiques to compliment his decor. The investment totaled one million dollars.

The Hudnuts enjoyed their Adirondack residence. They raised prize sheep and geese who were often seen wandering on the highway near their home. Mrs. Hudnut shopped in North Creek using her special carriage and prize team of horses. She was a large woman who had no use for the early cars and did her shopping by never leaving her carriage. She sent her coachman into each store to get what she needed. Local residents turned out in the streets on her shopping days to watch the coachman run in and out of the stores.

The first Mrs. Hudnut died and Richard married Winifred Shaughnessy whose daughter was the dancing partner and wife of the actor Rudolph Valentino. Rudolph came often to stay at this remote Adirondack estate. He brought a French chef from his Rivera estate to cook in the Adirondacks.

Mrs. Hudnut inherited the property upon Richard's death and, choosing not to live there, leased it to the Police Athletic League of New York City for a boys' camp in 1938. Four years later the PAL purchased it and operated a camp for six hundred boys each summer. They added a $25,000 recreation building in 1948 while spending $45,000 a year on maintenance. The camp was directed by Frank Campbell and the superintendents were Harry Armstrong and Roy Dunkley. Fred Gilbert was caretaker.

Fox Lair came to an end in the 60's when the State of New York purchased the now-defunct camp and returned the land to the wilderness. Nothing is left on the vast estate but a few foundations and the replanted evergreen trees. Another Adirondack enterprise has become a part of the "forever wild" Adirondacks.

THE RHINELANDER ESTATE

Philip Rhinelander, Jr. had a dream. He envisioned a vast baronial estate on lands in Hamilton County acquired by his grandfather, Frederick Rylander, in 1786. They came off the famous Totten and Crossfield Purchase. Philip pictured a village developing where present-day Speculator sits—a short distance from his Elm Lake holdings. He wisely purchased fifty acres at the Speculator site for less than $300 in anticipation of future development.

Philip was out-of-place with the few settlers in the rural Adirondack country. College-educated Philip had studied at Columbia College and in England and was a member of the New York State Bar. His huge mansion and three hundred-acre stock farm manned by servants and slaves was foreign to the rural Adirondacks of 1815.

Philip came from a well-to-do family. His Protestant ancestors had come to America in 1636 with the Huguenots. They did well in the new land and Philip used the wealth to purchase Adirondack land. He speculated on lands along the new state highway and enticed the town fathers to build a public road to his estate.

Philip built a luxurious mansion. The bricks used in the building were made on a site across Elm Lake. The rooms were oversized and finished with mahogany and adorned with beautiful paintings.

The grounds were developed with a cut-stone terrace and a park. An orchard supplied apples, plums, pears, and grapes. Stables, carriage houses, a creamery, outhouses, and barns were added to the estate. The laundry was done in a nearby stream. A sawmill and a gristmill were constructed at the Lake Pleasant outlet. One hundred acres were planted in crops in what is Adirondack wilderness today. The pasture lands took care of cattle, horses, sheep, and oxen.

Philip became active in the growing community. He served in various positions including assessor, commissioner of schools, overseer of highways, election inspector, supervisor, and representative of Montgomery County (included Hamilton County until 1835) to the New York State Constitutional Convention of 1821.

Philip married Mary Colden Hoffman and had a son and a daughter. The son died a bachelor at the age of twenty-four, ending any chance of taking over his father's massive Adirondack estate.

Philip was unduly possessive of his beautiful wife and she became a "prisoner" in her Adirondack home. There are many stories of her attempts to communicate with the outside world only to have her message intercepted or the messenger found dead.

Whether the stories of Mary Rhinelander's life were true or not, she had an unhappy existence in her great mansion. She became ill within three years of the move to Elm Lake and passed away in the autumn of 1818. Stories of slow poisoning circulated among the suspicious townspeople.

Philip built a large brick vault near the mansion to keep his wife's body during the winter. The ceiling was painted with a scene of "Resurrection Morning." In the spring the body was taken to New York City for eventual burial in St. Paul's churchyard.

Philip remained at his baronial estate until 1823. He was in his second term as supervisor and had immersed himself in his community activities and running his estate. A sudden paralysis ended his Adirondack career. He left for New York City and never returned. He passed away in 1830.

The estate was occupied by Thomas Wayne from England for a few years. After 1828 the once stately mansion was boarded up and watched over by a caretaker. It also became "haunted" at this time.

The stories grew. Workers hired to get in the hay for the animals still on the farm would sometimes spend the night in the mansion. Mrs. Rhinelander was seen walking about and sobbing with grief. A man in riding boots was heard walking on the stairs. Bedclothes were pulled off and dragging bodies were heard. A ghost was seen walking into the huge fireplaces. Other weird occurrences added to the tales and no one wanted to stay at the estate.

The end was in sight. Furniture was sold off to help pay delinquent taxes. The land was sold off; today it is owned by International Paper Company. Philip's daughter, who lived in New York City, gave a lot to the village to erect a schoolhouse. It is the site of the Speculator cemetery. Other holdings were sold to local residents. The Rhinelanders had cut their ties to the Adirondacks.

A tragic fire around 1875 erased the evidence of Philip's great dream of a baronial estate in the Adirondacks. The abandoned mansion was burned to the ground. Outbuildings were left to decay. Today, only the ruins and a few bricks can be found among the fast-growing trees and bushes of the Adirondacks.

XII

Adirondack Writers

GEORGE TIBBITTS—
THE MYSTERY OF KUNJAMUCK CAVE

Those who row or canoe up the Kunjamuck River near Speculator pass a small trail to a local historic spot, Kunjamuck Cave. It is a fair-size cave that once brought the promise of instant wealth to gold and silver miners, precious mineral collectors and amateur prospectors. The promise was as empty as the cave; nothing of worth developed except the creation of a nice cave to visit and to tell stories about.

The Mystery of Kunjamuck Cave is one of the stories centered around this Adirondack cave. Written in 1928 by an unknown author, George F. Tibbitts, it is a "strange mystery that leads like a will-o-wisp on a trail through the beautiful mountain and lake country of the Adirondacks." Information on the book jacket explains, "the book in a very true sense reveals the forces that are at work in the world to uplift and redeem, and also the forces that are ever active to enslave and destroy mankind."

The Mystery of Kunjamuck Cave tells of a New York businessman who came to the Great North Woods for rest and outdoor recreation. He gets involved in a mystery with French Louie as a central figure. Other characters were based on local residents with thinly disguised names. Uncle Dave in the story was believed to be Dave Sturges, Milt Boyd was possibly Milton Buyce, and Isaiah Pike was likened to Isaiah Perkins, and so on. Apparently Tibbitts lived in the area and wrote from his knowledge of the region and its people, including a reference to the old FJ&G railroad station at Northville.

Who was this author who knew the Adirondacks so well? His name may sound familiar to some of our readers. George Tibbitts was none other than "Pop" Tibbitts, founder of the Camp-of-the-Woods at Speculator. Pop Tibbitts, highly successful YMCA Director, was one who appreciated the value of an Adirondack experience. With his 319-page book and his camp he sought to share his Adirondacks with others.

George got an early start in the world of work; he left his home at the age of sixteen to get away from an alcoholic father. He began "Y" work in Detroit and, loving music, he sold pianos and organs. He saved his money and studied piano, organ, and conducting at the Boston Conservatory of Music.

Unfortunately, the hardworking George was struck by tuberculosis. He moved to Colorado for three years to rid himself of the disease. He was back at work in 1889 serving YMCA's in New York City, Cincinnati, Lynchburg, Washington, D.C., and Johnstown, New York.

George developed an interest in camping during his work with the Y. He believed in camping ministry. His interest led to the founding of Camp Dudley, the first of the YMCA camps. He helped to found the conference center at Silver Bay on Lake George. His camp at Glen Eyrie on Lake George thrived in the early 1900's.

George loved to camp in the Adirondacks. One of his camping partners was Charles B. Knox of Knox Gelatin. On one of their trips they observed the church steeples in the Lake Pleasant-Speculator area and decided to "build an alter to Jehovah on the shores of Lake Pleasant." The Adirondacks had captured Pop Tibbitts and the rest of his life was intertwined with the beauty of the mountains and lakes.

By 1917 George had arranged to purchase fifty acres on the shores of Lake Pleasant from two families named Slack. He wanted a "camp of the woods where city dwellers could enjoy the beauty and health-giving qualities of the Adirondacks as a living testimony to the glory of the divine."

Pop Tibbitts devoted his energies to his summer camp, Camp-of-the-Woods, and to his winter camp, Park-of-the-Palms in Florida. He built them into highly successful outdoor religious camps where thousands come each year. He died in 1948 and passed the reins to his secretary and friend, Gordon Purdy. Camp-of-the-Woods became a year-round operation in 1966 and Park-of-the-Palms was sold.

Pop Tibbitts was a unique Adirondacker. He loved the lakes and mountains and found a way to share them with others. His camp and his book stand as monuments to his life and the Adirondacks which he made a positive force in the lives of his people.

AMERICAN HERITAGE—ADIRONDACK READINGS

Over the years the Adirondacks have occasionally hit the national scene by appearing in major magazine articles. It is important that someone takes the time to write down a bit of the history and lore of the Adirondacks and, in some cases, it is the only source of information that we have on some Adirondack subjects. One of the magazines which recognizes the Adirondacks is the *American Heritage* and there are three editions which I refer to as the "Adirondack Editions."

My favorite *American Heritage* magazine was published in August of 1969. The cover is an 1878 lithograph of the Reverend W.H.H. "Adirondack" Murray. Murray wrote the book, *Adventures in the Wilderness*, which opened up the Adirondacks in 1869 and caused a rush of visitors far beyond the ability of the area to handle. The lithograph is unique in that it contains some subliminal advertising. A careful observer can see "Saranac Gloves" hidden in the shimmering waters of the lake.

The *Heritage* article on the Adirondacks covers the highpoints of man's discovery of New York's High Peaks. It marked the beginning of *American Heritage's* concern for our national heritage as well as our historical heritage.

Over a dozen pages in the *Heritage* "Adirondack Edition" are devoted to color pictures of some of the finest Adirondack paintings. Thomas Cole, Arthur Fitzwilliam Tait, and Winslow Homer are among the Adirondack artists who recorded the Adirondacks for posterity. And Harper's 1870 *New Monthly Magazine* "before-and-after" cartoon of the Adirondack vacationer appears in a woodcut. The magazine is a collector's item.

Another of my favorite "Adirondack Editions" of the *American Heritage* was published in April of 1965. It contains an article on one of the first Adirondack guides who was also a hero of the Revolution and the War of 1812. Frederick B. Leach of New Jersey wrote an article on Fulton County's folk hero, Nicholas Stoner, with the title "The Man Who Praises We Sing." His article was based on the writings of Mohawk Valley historian, Jeptha Simms. It contains a reference to the old Gloversville High School football fight song describing Nick Stoner. Leach concluded that even though Nick's warts are large, he belongs to Fulton County and "no amount of setting the record straight will dim his luster there!" (I added to his luster in my 1969 book.)

Another *Heritage* "Adirondack Edition," dated April 1973, contains an article on the "Gracious Record of a Connecticut Family" by Joan Kerr. The story takes place in the 1880's when the Hotchkiss family of New Haven had a summer camp in the Adirondacks. Henry, the father, had a camera and recorded their adventures on glass photographic plates. They have been preserved.

The Hotchkiss men began with a hunting camp near Upper St. Regis Lake, which evolved to tents on platforms and finally to elegant log cabins. The same scenario was repeated by many of those who could afford it in the early days of Adirondack history.

The photographs are priceless. The hunting party picture includes the well-dressed sports, the guides, the guideboat, the packbaskets, and the game. The cabin picture includes the huge native stone fireplace, the log beams, and mounted moose head. The tent photo is a classic. It includes all the comforts of home; the carpet, cots, tables and cupboards, and growing plants. The pictures tell Adirondack stories in themselves.

Other *American Heritage* magazines, for example October and December of 1963, are somewhat Adirondacky. They tell the story of the Revolutionary War which touched on the Adirondacks. Lake George and Lake Champlain played an important role and it has been recorded in the pages of *American Heritage*.

It is magazines such as the *American Heritage* which add to our understanding of the Adirondack region and add to the body of literature for future generations. And, as Murray found out, we should never underestimate the power of the printed word.

GERTRUDE ATHERTON—NOVELIST

The letter came from "Boulder Lake, The Great North Woods, Hamilton County, New York, USA" in June of 1900. It was written by Lady Helen Pole to her friend in England, the Countess of Edge and Ross. It was the first of a series of nine, rather lengthy, letters relating the Lady Helen's impressions of a sojourn in the Adirondacks. Obviously, they were written by someone who spent time in New York's great wilderness.

The descriptions in the letters are strictly Adirondack and could only have been written by one who had some firsthand knowledge of Adirondack life at the turn of the century. A look at some of the most obvious observations by the writer include:

THE GREAT CAMP: "It is built of big logs, with the rough bark on, and an upper and lower veranda connected by little flights of stairs. Inside it is "sealed" with diagonal strips of polished wood instead of plaster; the floors are also of hardwood with rugs, and the furniture is mostly rustic. In the living room is a huge fireplace of stones with the moss on. The low ceiling is crossed with heavy beams and there are several mounted deer-heads."

AN ADIRONDACK GROTTO: "Best of all I have discovered a gorge, sloping gently on one side, the other a huge boulder covered with moss; in the bottom of the gorge a brook pushing its tortuous way over rocks; and alders and ferns close to the banks."

THE MOUNTAIN: "It is Nature, virgin and ignorant, and it often gives me the most unaccountable sensation."

FOREVER WILD: "Civilisation [sic] is held in check at present by the laws of New York which owns the greater portion of the Adirondack tract. But for how long?"

THE ADRIONDACK FARMER: "But they are pale and thin and stooping, not one looks as if he would see sixty or as if he got the least pleasure out of life."

THE ADIRONDACK LEAN-TO: "Have you wasted any time imagining what an "open camp" is like? The briefest description will fit it. Three sides and a sloping roof, all of bark."

ADIRONDACK TROUT: "The men returned soon after with a basket full of trout and we fried them for supper. I don't think I ever eat anything quite so good as those trout."

Who was this Helen Pole from across the sea who knew so much about the Adirondacks? Was she really who she claimed to be? No, Helen Pole was a pseudonym used by American writer Gertrude Atherton. Gertrude had fallen into disfavor with American publishers and used her English subterfuge to get to the American public. It worked. She became an accepted American writer with over sixty novels to her credit when she died in 1948 at the age of ninety.

Gertrude had an unsettled childhood; the product of a broken home. Sent off to boarding school by her stepfather she became engaged to two men at the same time. Excluded from school, she returned home to steal her mother's new boyfriend, George Atherton, wealthy rancher, and to marry him.

Gertrude was unhappy with the responsibilities of home and children and turned to her writing. Upon the death of George at sea she abandoned her children and home and went to New York City to pursue her writing career.

Gertrude's novels, somewhat risque for her day, and with her radical ideas, were not popular with American critics. She called upon women to free themselves from the tyranny of men; it was the earliest proclamation by a female American author for women's liberation. Hence, her journey to England to establish herself and to get published.

Gertrude's 1902 Adirondack novel, entitled *The Aristocrats*, revealed her opinions on the "class" society in America and the role of women. She complained that the men got to do all the fun things at camp such as hunting and fishing. The women were relegated to the porches to play cards and read or to take a short walk near the camp.

The Aristocrats was well-accepted by the critics and received good reviews in America. It became a bestseller and remains today as one of the most descriptive works of life in the heydays of the Adirondacks.

JOHN BURROUGHS—NATURALIST

Well-known naturalist John Burroughs visited Gloversville, the Adirondacks' gateway city, sometime after 1910. He was a guest at the Nature Study Club named in his honor. The Burroughs Club, now in its 82nd year, still meets today.

The Gloversville trip was not Burroughs' first trip to upstate New York. In the summer of 1863 the noted teacher had made a trip to the wilds of the Adirondacks. The twenty-six-year-old nature lover recorded his Adirondack impressions in *Wake Robin*, Volume I of his *Works*. "Wake-robin" is a name for trillium, a flower that blooms when the birds return in the spring. Burroughs hiked the Adirondacks in search of birds.

Interestingly, Burroughs wrote about the Adirondacks while serving as a watchman in the United States Treasury vault at Washington, D.C. Writing helped to kill time during the long hours on a boring job.

Chapter III of *Wake Robin* holds the title, "Adirondac." Burroughs wrote during the period of history when the "k" was dropped from the end of Adirondack. He was pursuing the study of birds at the time and was curious about what could be found in the Adirondack wilderness. He was disappointed; he found nothing "rare and precious."

Burroughs entered the Adirondacks through the Lake George region. He stayed with an old pioneer and hunter, Hewett (possibly Hulett). Hewett's son, Bub, served as guide and took the bird watcher to the Stillwater of the Boreas, a branch of the Hudson River, in today's

Town of Minerva.

The party stayed in an old lumberman's shanty and took trout from the Stillwater. Burroughs caught a half dozen after the guide had failed. He reported that from this point on the guide treated him "with the tone and freedom of a comrade and equal!" Burroughs described a cave near the same spot that contained a warm outlet stream from a lake on the top of a mountain.

Burroughs wanted to try deer hunting which was commonly done on the lakes in those days. The guide took them up a mountain to Bloody-Moose-Pond (today's Moose Pond). They spotted a blue heron but no deer, so they pressed on to Nate's Pond.

The guide suggested that the group stay at the hunter's cabin at the far end of the lake. Burroughs described it as "approved style, three sides enclosed, with a roof of bark and a bed of boughs, and a rock in front that afforded a permanent back-log to all fires." It was an early Adirondack lean-to.

The search was made for a dugout canoe which usually could be found near the Adirondack Lakes. It was located and patched up so that the party could "float" for their venison. A jack-light with three candles was mounted on a stick at the front of the craft. Serious hunting was done at night .

Burroughs spent half the night in the front of the boat with the gun and, after some adventure, shot a doe. He was not a hunter and reported, "the success was but an indifferent one..." When it came time to eat the venison "it was black and strong."

Burroughs reported seeing a couple dozen different birds on his Adirondack bird hunt. He mentioned the hermit thrush, reporting large numbers on Lake Sandford (Sanford) in the raspberry patches. A local farm boy told him they were "partridge-birds" because they sounded like partridge.

Their trip took them to the Lower Iron Works and on to Long Lake, where they found a welcomed hotel. The MacIntyre mining operation had ceased and Burroughs described the abandoned remains. He met the caretaker and his family who lived at the Upper Works, twenty-five miles from anything.

Burroughs' enjoyment of the Adirondack wilds went beyond fish and game and scenery and adventure. He found the "wordless intercourse with rude Nature" to be the best part of the expedition. He knew the "health and vigor in her veins."

IRVING BACHELLER—NOVELIST

One of the best Adirondack historical novels ever written became a runaway best seller at the turn of the century and is still selling today. It has been printed and reprinted over the years and well over one million copies have been sold. The book is Irving Bacheller's *Eben Holden, A Tale of the North Country*.

Irving Addison Bacheller was destined to become a writer. He was named after Washington Irving, the first of America's great writers (whose sisters lived and died in Johnstown), and after Joseph Addison, an English writer. Irving died in 1859, the year Bacheller was born.

Bacheller began his life working on his father's farm in upstate New York and clerking in the village store. He was scholarly inclined and obtained an education degree from St. Lawrence University. (There is hope for me: I began life working on my father's farm in upstate New York and clerking in Mosher's general store in Northville. I received my education degree from SUNY Plattsburgh.) Bacheller also was awarded five honorary degrees.

At the beginning of his journalistic career Bacheller went to New York City to work for the newspapers of the day. He founded the first American newspaper syndicate and published the works of some of the famous writers of his time. He became a friend of Stephen Crane and Mark Twain. They founded the Lanthorne Literary Club.

Bacheller became a member of the Century Club, Authors' Club of New York, New York Society of Mayflower Descendents, Sons of the Revolution, New England Society of New York, and the Masons. He received the Grand Masonic Lodge of New York State medal for his contribution to the fine arts.

In 1816 Bacheller sold his newspaper syndicate to become editor of *The Pocket Magazine*, a world Sunday paper. Three years later he retired at the age of forty to become a full-time writer. He also became a folk singer, a public speaker, and completed over thirty novels during the next fifty years. He died in New York City in 1950. Bacheller's novels specialized in rural scenes, wholesome living, and Abraham Lincoln. His songs and poems were dispersed throughout his novels.

Bacheller revealed that the characters in his books were mostly men and women he had known. One of his characters, Silas Strong, was based on Philo (Fide) Scott, his favorite Adirondack guide. This novel written in 1906, entitled *Silas Strong, Emperor of the Woods*, was "nothing more than a simple account of one summer's life, pretty much as it was lived, in a part of the Adirondacks."

Bacheller showed his concern for the Adirondack woods in the *Silas Strong* novel. He speaks of Silas losing his wilderness "empire." He tried to tell the "sad story of the wilderness itself—to show it from the woodsman's viewpoint, the play of great forces which have been tearing down his home and turning it into the flesh and bone of cities." He hoped that his readers would value what remains of the forest. He wanted to check the "greed of the saws."

Eben's role in the novel was that of the wise bachelor uncle of the teller of the tale. His Adirondack exploits were unsurpassed. He left us with some words to live by when going to his grave:

> "I ain't afraid
> 'Shamed o' nuthin' I ever done
> Alwuss kep' my tugs tight,
> Never swore 'less 'twas nec'sary,
> Never ketched a fish bigger'n 'twas
> Er lied 'n a hoss trade
> Er shed a tear I didn't hev to."

BARNEY FOWLER—COLUMNIST

Remember Barney Fowler? Barney was one of a kind. He loved the Adirondacks and spent a lifetime writing about them. He spent half a century writing over 15,000 columns. His photographs were priceless. My scrapbooks of Barney's work measure over half a foot in thickness.

Barney Fowler began in newspaper work in the 1930's. Whatever he did he always returned to the Adirondacks. He expressed his opinion on every Adirondack issue. He experienced every issue firsthand before taking his stand. He traveled the waters of the Adirondacks to speak out on boating regulations. He climbed the trailless peaks to form his opinions. He opposed the Gooley Dam project on the upper Hudson only after his own field investigation. He always did his homework.

Barney Fowler is a part of my "Adirondack Education." He has written about more Adirondack subjects than any I know. His three books, *Adirondack Albums*, contain some of his photos and research. His outdoor columns over the years would fill volumes. No Adirondack subject was too remote to appear under his pen.

Those who followed Barney Fowler's writings soon learned his "pet" names for those he wrote about. His dog was "World's Greatest Set of Living Teeth." He called his car "The Mouse" and referred to his readers as "Murgatoyd or Mowgli." The legislature was Baloney Hill and one of the state departments was "The State Office of Parks and Wreckreation." New York State became "My Big Brother the Bookie." The taxpayer was "The Man In The Barrel" and the Northway was the "Trail of Torture." He had several others but the greatest was himself "The Old Curmudgeon." His sense of humor included himself knowing that many enjoy referring to him as a gruff old man.

It was not difficult to know where Barney Fowler stood on Adirondack issues. He supported the Environmental Conservation Department and the Adirondack Park Agency. But, let them do something wrong and he let his readers know about it. He opposed the use of snowmobiles on Forest Preserve lands but he agreed to ride on one for charity.

It was not uncommon for a man of Barney's stature to be recognized for his love and advocacy for the Adirondacks. He was the Conservation Communicator of the Year for the New York State Conservation Council, National Wildlife Federation, and the Sears-Roebuck Foundation in 1967. The Police Benevolent Association honored him twice. The Forest Rangers have honored him as well as the Lake Champlain Committee. He was honored during the Centennial of the Forest Preserve. The Scripps-Howard Newspapers gave him the National Conservation Award. He was well-known and well-liked. His crusades earned him the respect of many.

Barney added public speaking and a radio show to his accomplishments over the years. He once sent me a note telling how impressed he was with my first book on Nick Stoner. I invited him up to speak to the Gloversville Lions Club and we had a good talk on his fifty years of hiking, camping, canoeing, and fishing the Adirondacks. He skied at North Creek in the 1930's and made friends with the Russian newsmen at the 1980 Olympics. Barney did what he best describes himself "... preserve our basic love for the North Country with a newsman's viewpoint."

Barney once said that nobody knows all that there is about the Adirondacks. We can agree with that and we can also agree that Barney's love and concern for the region that we call the Adirondacks stands out in history. Barney Fowler will live on in his writings and will long be remembered by those who share his Adirondacks.

MAITLAND DeSORMO—HISTORIAN

We lost an Adirondack "giant" this year. Maitland C. DeSormo passed away in Saranac Lake in his eighty-sixth year. He taught high school English for forty of his eighty-six years and, more than that, he taught us all about the Adirondacks.

Mait loved the Adirondacks. He loved to tell Adirondack stories and to converse at length with other Adirondackers. He wrote his first Adirondack book when he was sixty years old and went on to write or edit several other books, most of which were on Adirondack subjects. Mait also published over seventy-five Adirondack articles and worked on endless television, radio, and slide show Adirondack programs. He stood tall when it came to New York's Adirondack region.

Mait DeSormo was usually highly visible at Adirondack gatherings. He and his wife owned Adirondack Yesteryears, an Adirondack publishing and sales company. He was historian for the town of Harrietstown and past-president of the Lake Placid-North Elba Historical Society. Mait joined the Adirondack Mountain Club, the Wilderness Society, and climbed all of the Adirondack's forty-six High Peaks. He won several awards during his Adirondack "career" including an honorary doctorate from St. Lawrence University.

Mait's books comprise an Adirondack library by themselves. *Told Around the Campfire* tells the tale of an early Adirondack entrepreneur/ hotel keeper, Henry van Hoevenburg. *Noah John Rondeau, Adirondack Hermit* is a classic biography, well-researched, on the Adirondack's most famous hermit. *Seneca Ray Stoddard, Versatile Camera-Artist* provides the information needed to understand and appreciate the many-sided talents of an Adirondack photographer and guidebook writer of the 1800's.

Old Times in the Adirondacks, The Heydays of the Adirondacks, and *Summers on the Saranac* contain a wealth of Adirondack history, stories, and photographs. Mait collected the details on roads, railroads, lean-tos, hotels, guides, lumbering, and other Adirondack topics and wove the stories and yarns into his masterful manuscripts. Future generations can re-live the heydays of the Adirondacks through DeSormo's writings.

Mait's last book, *The Murray Rush in Retrospect* is a study of W.H. H. "Adirondack" Murray's best seller of 1869, *Adventures in the Wilderness*. The controversial and charismatic Reverend Murray is the subject of a "consensus composite" by DeSormo. The book also contains a section on Maitland's wit and humor; "wit to make you think and humor to make you laugh."

Mait penned a note on "Nostalgia" in his final book calling it a tricky emotion, a regret for lost youth when "dreams came easy and lingered long." He also penned personal notes to me in autographed copies of his books which I will always cherish. Mait became part of my support network calling me "another reputable Adirondack author," "a competent Adirondack historian and fine fellow besides," "an Adirondack addict and writer of distinction," and a word of advice, "keep the scripts coming." I try!

EMILY POST—ETIQUETTE

When we think of Emily Post we think etiquette. How then, did Emily Post, author of the most successful book of etiquette ever written, get an Adirondack connection? Can it be true that the first lady of manners and high society found her way into the turn-of-the-century Adirondacks?

'Tis true. Emily Post enjoyed a sojourn at an Adirondack "camp." Those who know the Adirondacks know that a "camp" can be a one-room shanty or a giant wealthy estate. The Great Camps of the Adirondacks were just that; they were the summer homes of some of America's wealthiest families. And Emily Post needed to write a chapter on the proper behavior at an Adirondack camp.

When the Post book was reprinted in the early '20's a chapter, "The House Party in Camp" was included among the usual chapters on "Teas and Other Afternoon Parties," "Balls and Dances," "Clothes of a Gentleman," and "Everyday Manners at Home." Vacationers were "roughing it" in the mountains and Mrs. Post wanted to give them guidance in manners and morals.

Many problems needed to be resolved. Do you take your maid or valet to camp? According to Mrs. Post, some did and some did not. Clothes were a specialty; the men rummaged through attics and trunkrooms for those articles of wearing apparel dear to all sportsmen: oil-soaked boots, water-soaked and sun-bleached woolen, corduroy, leather, or canvas garment and hats. Guns had to be cleaned and fishing equipment gathered.

The women had a real problem with dress. Much had to be eliminated without a maid's help to get into or to take care of. Skirts, sweaters, and lots of plain shirt waists were recommended. Old polo coats or a mackintosh was necessary. A house gown or day dress was required for the evenings at camp. Plain tea gowns in dark color were also included. Women were also required to take something to work on such as sewing or knitting for the hours of sitting while the men fished.

The train ride to camp took some eight to eighteen hours. The group was met at the station by two buckboards and an express wagon to take them over a "corduroy" road some six to eight miles to the camp. The camp appeared to Emily to be a group of log buildings "dumped in a clearing among the pine trees."

Mrs. Post described the camp in detail. She pictures the dining room and the one cloth napkin per day rule. A list of amusements is included for the camp guest. The use of guides, swimming options, boats to use, and just sitting in the hammock or on a divan are among the choices.

An appreciation for the work involved in running a great camp is evident in Mrs. Post's writing. "A dozen guides, teams and drivers, natives to wash and clean and to help the cook; food for two or three dozen people sent hundreds of miles by express!"

In camp, according to Mrs. Post, people do not "dress" for dinner, that is, not in evening clothes. Women put on their house gowns, men put on flannel trousers, soft shirts, and serge sack coats. The evening was spent around an outside fire in good weather and at the fireplace when stormy.

Emily Post admits that etiquette may not belong or be needed in camp. "The etiquette of this sort of party is so apparently lacking that its inclusion perhaps seems out of place." She included it in her book to show that well-bred people "never deteriorate in manners." Their behavior is precisely the same whether at great estates or at great camps. However, she did mention one lady who wore a squirrel fur hat in the evening as well as the daytime because it was so "warm and comfortable." It was really because she could not do her hair without a maid!

JOHN TODD—MINISTER

The Adirondacks have a long history of religious circuit riders, missionaries, itinerant preachers, and priests who traversed New York's frontier. They brought the word of God to a godless wilderness.

The early Adirondack settlers, scattered throughout the wilderness, separated by miles of forested lands and high mountains, followed similar patterns of growth. The speculators brought in the families to farm the lands and to establish the industries. Grist mills and lumber mills became a necessity. Town fathers solicited a piece of land for the school house. And, sooner or later, life in the Adirondacks raised the need for a church.

Circuit riders brought the Word of God to the isolated Christians and strived to save the heathen. The hardships experienced by the early men of God in the Adirondacks is a matter of record. There are stories of those lost in the wilderness, beaten, and drowned in the rushing waters. The Adirondacks were as tough a mission as any found in foreign lands.

Possibly the earliest clergyman of record to traverse the Adirondack wilderness was the Reverend John Todd of Pittsfield, Massachusetts. In 1841 the Reverend Todd was invited to speak at the commencement exercises at Burlington College (today's University of Vermont). He saw the "horizon of mountains" across Lake Champlain "where Nature walks alone" and decided that he wanted to visit them.

One of the professors at Burlington, Farrand N. Benedict, had spent seven years exploring the Adirondacks and developing his interests in the wilderness. He invited Todd to join his party for an Adirondack trip. Thus, in August of 1841, the Reverend John Todd began a serious relationship with the East's greatest wilderness.

The Reverend Todd saw the need for missionary work at Long Lake. In the spring of 1842 he spoke in Boston about the need for good books and possibly a missionary in the Adirondacks. He returned each summer and continued writing letters to the newspapers to get support. He collected funds for books and medicine. The children of his Sunday School raised enough money for a six-week missionary. Missionary Parker answered the call and stayed for more than a year, supported by the settlers. Noted journalist, Joel T. Headley, met Parker and observed, "Parker is strong and vigorous, just the man for such a place."

The Reverend Todd was also a man for the Adirondacks. He spent his boyhood in the out-of-doors and was well-versed in woodcraft. He was an avid deer hunter and enjoyed challenging the wild waters of the Adirondacks in a canoe.

Todd wrote one of the earliest Adirondack books. In 1845 his recollections of Long Lake were printed by E. P. Little in Pittsfield. He provided a clear picture of life in the primeval Adirondacks. The book has been reprinted for today's readers.

On his first trip in 1841, Todd tells of finding eight or nine families scattered along towards the head of Long Lake. They lived in log cabins and used small boats for transportation. Physicians and stores were fifty miles away by footpath. They lived on moose, deer, and trout.

Todd found eleven families on his second annual visit totaling some sixty people. He was surprised to find that they had formed a temperance society and a Sabbath School. It was during this visit in 1842, 150 years ago, that the Reverend Todd organized eleven of the Adirondack settlers into "the First Congregational Church on Long Lake".

On the third visit Todd predicted that the Adirondacks would someday be inhibited by over a million. He envisioned prosperous Christian communities springing up once the forests were cut down. On this 1843 visit Todd also found that his package of books and medicines had arrived in the settlement during a December rainstorm and the anxious citizens of Long Lake waded the wet lake to get them. A schoolhouse had been constructed which provided a place of assembly. It was during this trip that land was donated for a church. Plans for a road from Lake Champlain were made by the state.

On one of his trips the Reverend Todd visited with the son of an Abenaki chief, Sabael, who lived near Indian Lake. He described Sabael's wigwam, "no floor, no table, no chair, or bed!" Todd questioned Sabael about his beads, which he reported were given to him by a priest. Sabael said that they kept him safe from harm and he lived to be 106.

Who was Sabael's priest? Was there another holy man who penetrated the godless wilderness with the Reverend Todd?

XIII

Adirondack Mysteries and Crime

AN AMERICAN TRAGEDY

Theodore Dreiser wrote *An American Tragedy* in the early twenties. Published in 1925, it was expected to become America's contribution to the world's literature. The rather lengthy novel, written in two parts, was based on a true story of a murder in the Adirondacks. It never quite reached the acclaim that Dreiser had expected. The true story, however, captivated Adirondackers for several months.

When Oliver Whitman wrote in his Adirondack journals he recorded little of the "outside world." But on April 3, 1908, he took the time to note some important news, "Gilette was lectreculd March the 30 in the morning for kiling Grace Brown."

The Gillette murder trial had been the subject of great interest since July of 1906 when the body of Grace (Billy) Brown was found in the bottom of Big Moose Lake in the Adirondacks. Her worldly boyfriend, Chester Gillette, was accused of her murder.

Adirondack communities were well-settled by the first decade of the present century and excitement, such as what the Gillette trial brought to the area, was the talk of the towns. When Gillette came to trial at the County Court House in Herkimer in November of 1906, crowds of people surrounded the place shouting, "Murderer! Brute!" Feelings ran high in the Adirondacks once the story surfaced.

Chester had taken his girlfriend, Grace, who was expecting his child, on a "honeymoon" trip to the Glenmore Hotel on Big Moose Lake near Tupper Lake. The couple went for a boat ride on the lake and never returned. Subsequently, Grace's body was brought from the bottom of the water and Chester had secretly left the area. A bruise on her head led to the finding of Chester's battered tennis racket in the woods and a month-long trial with 109 witnesses.

It was somewhat tragic that Chester's defense lawyer, ex-senator Albert M. Mills, did not find Roy Higby. Roy was thirteen years old when he was told to "keep your mouth shut." He was never called as a witness although he had some important information to tell. Chester Gillette would never have been electrocuted if Roy had told his story of seeing the body poked with pike poles before it was brought to the surface. Grace's head injury could have been caused by the metal end on the pole.

Chester knew the Adirondacks; he had been there before. He had made at least two trips up Black Bear Mountain. He had canoed Seventh Lake. He had dined at Frank Williams' Seventh Lake House. He knew the Inlet Inn (later Arrowhead Inn) at Eagle Bay where he went after leaving Grace in the lake.

Chester had planned the fatal trip well. He took Grace to a hotel in Utica, on to Tupper Lake to stay, and finally to the Glenmore Hotel on Big Moose. He registered himself as Carl Grahm and Charles Gordon, matching the C.G. initials on his suitcase.

The entire story, from beginning to end, made for a great novel. Dreiser made a few changes while following the basic story line. He called Chester, Clyde, and named Grace, Roberta. His story used a camera for the murder weapon. He linked Clyde (Chester) to another socialite increasing the motive for getting rid of Roberta (Grace).

The story was the subject of a radio play on the NBC University Theater in 1948. It has been the subject of several books, two motion pictures, two plays, a television program, magazine articles, student theses, and folk songs. The Adirondack tragedy has spread beyond the Blueline.

The final ending of this tragic story had an ironic twist. Some still believed that Grace had thrown herself in the water in despair and Chester was innocent. On the last day of Chester's life, March 21, 1908, Governor Charles Evans Hughes, upon the urgings of Chester's mother, called Auburn prison to ask for a stay of execution. He was assured by Warden Benham that "Chester Gillette confessed to his spiritual advisor and to the prison chaplain." That night he became the last man to be electrocuted at Auburn.

STRANGE ADIRONDACK MARKINGS

Wherever man goes his graffito follows. You can find it in the Adirondacks. Rocks and flat-faced rock cliffs attract those who cannot resist leaving their mark on time. Today's spray paint on a rock surface appears to last forever.

And we have the Adirondack pig. A huge rock between Speculator and Indian Lake on the Adirondack Trail, Route 30, resembles a pig. Nearby campers painted an eye and a pink nose on the rock several years ago and it became a landmark. When the road was being widened and improved in 1991, public outcry caused the State to clear around the rock and to leave it standing on a portion of the shoulder of the road.

Carvings in the rock provide another form of Adirondack graffito. They last forever. A "stagecoach" rock is found on Route 73, carved in the 1930's with a picture of an Adirondack stagecoach and horses. It perpetuates the memory of the Adirondack's early transportation system.

The western Adirondacks has its Sunday Rock. A huge rock that once was a gateway between the settlements and the wilderness became known as the Sunday Rock. Beyond the rock every day was Sunday. It was saved during some road construction in 1925 and a plaque was placed on it by the "Sunday Rock Association."

The Adirondacks also has its marks of mystery. Verplanck Colvin, Superintendent of the Adirondack Survey, left a rock message in Beaver River country. It was found early in the century under the leaves and moss and soon forgotten. In recent years it has been rediscovered, but still has an element of mystery.

Colvin carved his initials in the rock and the year of the survey, 1878. They are easily identified but other markings are subject to speculation. Carved on a rock bed, the markings take on a meaning when deciphered. The markings include N.Y., TC, 38A, Adk Sur, 1878, V.C., F.T., and McC along with an arrow pointing northeast.

The corner marked by the Colvin rock is the northwest corner of the Totten and Crossfield Purchase. Land titles of five million acres of Adirondack real estate depended upon locating this corner, important enough for the surveyor to engrave it.

Most of the markings are self-evident. Along with Colvin's initials and the date, the station number, New York, Totten and Crossfield, and Adirondack Survey are easily explained. F.T. are probably the intitials of the assistant in charge of that part of the survey, F. Tweedy. The McC is a mystery; one can only guess at its meaning.

Stone Bridge Caves, near Pottersville on Route 9, with its caves, grottos, pot holes, and 180-ft, natural stone bridge has its mystery. While walking the trails along the pools, caves, waterfalls, and rugged rock formations you will come across some ancient, apparently Spanish, carvings in the solid rock. No one knows when they appeared there or why. It is a mystery that, if solved, may bring new history to light about man's early exploration of the Adirondacks.

Another Adirondack graffito mystery is a strange symbol and letters found on Colvin Mountain. It may be another remnant of a Colvin survey but it is difficult to explain. A small triangle with a circle in the middle may be a bench mark. The letters O, C, A, and K are a mystery. Those initials are not listed in the record of Colvin's workers. One may speculate that the initials A. K. might be those of another Adirondack surveyor, Albert King of Speculator. He was in charge of all surveying of the southern half of the Adirondack Forest Preserve for the State of New York in the first part of this century. O. C. may have been a helper named Oswald, Orrin, Ora, or Orlando. Who knows?

Man has left these marks in the Adirondacks and there are probably others hidden in the vast forested wilderness to be found in some future time. The imprints of man on the immense wilderness are few and far between, but that is the way it should be in the "forever wild" Adirondacks.

THE "TELL-TALE" BILL

We like to think of the Adirondacks as a safe haven from the incessant urban crime reported on the nightly news. Unfortunately, the Adirondacks occasionally grab the headlines and become the focus of a dramatic crime. Public attention reaches its highest peak when it is an Adirondack crime.

The Gillette murder trial and the Garrow murders are well-known and gained worldwide attention in their day. Other, lesser-known crimes have trickled out of Adirondack history which remain in the minds of those who lived through the brief preoccupation of the public with every detail of the wrongdoings. The Duane/Davis case of the 1920's is one such crime which lingers in the memories of some of our older Adirondackers. They have never forgotten the ten-dollar bill with the hole in the middle!

Sixty-year old Eula Davis was a caretaker and guide for the property at Whitaker Lake near Speculator. He had made some money by guiding and harvesting the bounty of the Adirondack wilds and made the mistake of showing off his roll of bills. He was saving his money to buy a house on West Hill for his sister. Unfortunately, his $144 final payment was observed by thirty-four-year-old Ernest Duane, boxer

Gene Tunney's sometime guide.

Davis was found dead in his cabin. A bullet was lodged in his hip, having passed through his wallet. The corpse was taken out to Speculator so frozen that it took twelve hours to thaw for the autopsy. Seventeen pieces of currency were found in his flesh along with pieces of the bullet. Mysteriously, the cabin was destroyed by fire during the investigation.

The players in this case each added their special contribution to the conviction of Duane for the murder of Davis. Hamilton County had little need for an extensive legal system in those days. Governor Alfred E. Smith had to appoint a special prosecutor and require a Montgomery County judge to hold a special Supreme Court term.

Assistant District Attorney, Bernard (Pat) W. Kearney of Gloversville (later Congressman) asked for a verdict of murder.

Dr. Russell Warner of Wells, Dr. Harry Denham of Gloversville and Dr. Ward Cook, Littauer Hospital pathologist compared the currency fragments.

Duane's attorney, Carl McMahan of Saratoga Springs, defended the epileptic woodsman by declaring incompetency.

Duane's brother, Joe, who had gone into debt to hire the legal counsel, reported on his brother's "queer spells" and Dr. William Wright of Utica State Hospital called Duane a "ten year old."

Dr. John McDowell of Speculator reported that Duane had purchased life insurance without admitting to epileptic seizures.

Dr. William Shanahan of the Craig Colony for Epilepsy reported a man can have seizures and not be insane.

A firearms expert, Captain William A. Jones, verified the murder weapon was Duane's.

Amsterdam Supreme Court Justice Christopher R. Heffernan sentenced the guilty Duane to the electric chair.

Duane had made a major mistake. It appears that he had cashed a ten-dollar bill at the general store which had a hole in the middle and showed signs of bloodstains. A subsequent search of his home resulted in the finding of the rest of the money and the murder weapon. In essence, he convicted himself with the "tell-tale" bill.

The trial cost Hamilton County $15,000, the most costly in its day, and now Governor Franklin D. Roosevelt commuted the death sentence to life imprisonment. In 1950 Duane died on the operating table during a cyst operation on his head and is buried in Gloversville.

XIV

Adirondack Visitors

"INDIANS" IN THE ADIRONDACKS

Our knowledge of the Native Americans in our country has been tainted by Hollywood and, in many ways, it is difficult to separate fact from fiction. Such is the case with "Indians" in the Adirondacks. There are those whose imagination conjures up the image of the painted redman, dressed in loin cloth, moccasins and feathers, chasing game through the wild Adirondack Mountains with his bow and arrow. Some have him living in a teepee, the home used by the nomadic plains dwellers.

Archeological research sheds some light on the truth about the presence of Native Americans in the Adirondacks. Traces of the tribes who occasioned the Adirondacks for hunting and summer forays have been found. No tribe ever lived in the rugged mountainous country, although some peaks were named by and for them. Native Americans did not like the mountain tops and never went to their superstitious summits. The "Indians" were summer visitors much as many of us are today.

A record of individual Native Americans who chose to make their homes in the Adirondacks can be found. The first permanent settler in what is now Hamilton County was a Penobscot Indian, Sabael Benedict. Sound familiar? It should; it is the name of the small settlement this side of Indian Lake on Route 30. Indian Lake and Squaw Brook were so-named because of his presence. He was a good woodsman, living for six weeks at a time in the wilds of the Adirondacks.

Sabael began his long, 108 years, life on the Penobscot River in Maine. His family joined the Abenakis in Canada and at the age of twelve Sabael assisted the British during the 1759 Battle of Quebec. During the American Revolution, not wanting to fight his neighbors, he left his tribe and joined the patriot forces.

When the wars ceased Sabael ventured to the Adirondacks to settle down. He discovered Indian Lake, which at that time was three smaller lakes. It was, and is, good hunting, fishing, and trapping country and Sabael was able to survive with his squaw, his son, Lige (Lewis Elijah) and three daughters.

The Reverend John Todd visited the elder Benedict in 1852 and reported that his wigwam had a dirt floor which served as chair, table, and bed. He was over one hundred years old and still keen of eyesight and mind.

Sabael is credited with the discovery of the valuable iron ore deposit near Keesville. He told the Reverend Todd that he sold it for a bushel of corn and one dollar to some men from Broadalbin.

David Henderson, one of the buyers and owners of the Adirondack Iron and Steel Company, said that Sabael's son showed them the ore on the Hudson River near North Elba. Lewey Lake was named after this "strapping young Indian named Lewis Elijah." It is believed that Lewis was guiding Professor Ebenezer Emmons when he explored the high reaches of Mt. Marcy.

Sabael ended his long life in true Indian tradition. When he was visited in 1853 and found still in good health he had moved to the far side of Indian Lake to escape the ghosts. In 1855 at the age of 108 he made a trip to his hunting camp at Thirteenth Lake. He hiked into the Adirondack wilderness never to return.

Brief mention in history is made of another Indian Lake settler, John Camp, a member of Sabael's tribe. He may have been a son-in-law of Sabael. He was a sea captain for the British before he settled in the Adirondacks. His son, Elijah, became the first Native American to hold public office in the county. He became Overseer of the Poor in 1874, ending a history of the denial of voting rights and office holding by those considered non-citizens.

Another Adirondacker served on the side of the American Patriots during the Revolution. Peter Sabattis, also a member of Sabael's tribe and possibly a relative, served as a guide for Benedict Arnold's troops in their attack on Quebec in 1775. He continued his work as a scout during the Revolution and also the War of 1812. He retained his title of Captain for the remainder of his life.

Captain Sabattis was one of the earliest "summer residents" of Long Lake, spending summers there in the early 1800's. He died there at the age of 111, another tribute to the good life in the mountains.

Peter had three boys and a girl and one of his sons, Mitchell, became one of the earliest, permanent residents of Long Lake. He gained a wide reputation as an Adirondack Guide. His dog could trail and tree the wild Adirondack panther. He is credited with the development of the first Adirondack guide boat. His three sons also became guides.

Mitchell was a devoutly religious man and personally raised some $2,000 to build the Wesleyan Methodist Church in Long Lake. He led singing with his violin and became known as the "Reverend Mitchell" because of his preaching. The deed records that he purchased the church property for twenty-five dollars.

Stories of other "Indians" in the Adirondacks abound in the history of the region. There were the Thompsons and Brants in Long Lake. Captain Gill, a Mohawk Indian and friend of Nicholas Stoner, near Lake Pleasant. He was a devout Catholic who crossed himself whenever danger lurked in the wilderness. Pezeeko, a St. Regis Indian, lived on the western shore of the lake named after him, Piseco Lake.

Thus we find a story of "Indians" in the Adirondacks. It is a tale of a true relationship with the wilderness, a tale of a contribution to our country, and a tale of our fellow men with their struggles and heartbreaks, successes and happiness. And if you listen to the noise of the wind under the ice at Indian Lake you will hear the spirit of Sabael still roaming the wilderness he loved.

STARS IN THE ADIRONDACKS

The rich and famous have not been foreign to the forests and lakes of the Adirondacks; many have found the mountains to their liking over the years. Screen star Nedenia "Dina" Merrill, daughter of Marjorie Merriweather Post and E. F. Hutton, had her own cabin at the Post estate, Topridge, near Paul Smiths on St. Regis Lake. Her custom-made cottage with its pink interior, along with twenty other Topridge buildings has faced a series of owners in recent years.

Opera star Robert Merrill had his Adirondack beginnings. He quit school at age fifteen to work for his father. It was during the Depression and he was needed to keep the family business going. He was a shy boy who stuttered, yet he loved to sing. He took voice lessons during his lunchtime and after work, never dreaming that it would lead him to the Adirondacks and a lifelong career.

Passing Steinway Hall on 57th Street one day, Merrill found a crowd auditioning for a summer job at the Adirondack Resort, Sacroon Manor. He sang for the job and beat out the other forty.

At Sacroon Manor Merrill sang show tunes, backed up the chorus girls, and served as straight man for a new, young comedian, Red Skelton. The shyness and stuttering that he had known all of his life disappeared during his Adirondack days. Robert Merrill became a star in the

Adirondacks.

Kate Smith, America's favorite "God Bless America" singer, was an Adirondacker. She maintained a home on Buck Island on Lake Placid for over forty years, passing away in June of 1986. Camp Sunshine, as she called it, was the place she wanted to be. In the 1940's her radio show was broadcast from a small room over the boathouse, the world's smallest radio studio according to Ripley's "Believe It or Not."

Kate loved the Adirondacks and the people who lived there. She was down-to-earth and enjoyed the company of fun-loving people. Around Lake Placid she was known as a tee-totaller who never went to cocktail parties. She preferred milk mixed with Coca-Cola.

Kate, whose real name was Kathryn, became a Roman Catholic in 1965 and joined St. Agnes' Church in Lake Placid. She is still there today, entombed in a pink granite mausoleum in the church cemetery. It was her wish to be buried in the Adirondacks and after some controversy and a seventeen month wait on the size of the tomb, it was accomplished. Efforts are underway today to turn her Adirondack complex into a Kate Smith museum.

Rudolph Valentino, star of the silent screen, had his day in the Adirondacks. He married his dancing partner, the daughter of Winifred Shanghnessy, Richard Hudnut's second wife. Rudolph enjoyed the life at the family's Adirondack estate at Fox Lair near Bakers Mills. He enjoyed the outdoor life along with the elaborate estate with its imported French furniture and French chef from the Rivera.

Not all stars publicize their Adirondack connections. There are many we seldom hear about who vacation or own homes in the Adirondacks. Kamp Kill Kare, near Raquette Lake, built by Lt. Gov. William Woodruff in 1897, is rumored to be owned by an anonymous young starlet. The property had been purchased and expanded by the Frances Garvan family in 1914 and sold to the present owner in the early '80's. The remoteness of the Adirondack forests also serves to hide the stars and to preserve the privacy of those who desire seclusion from the outside world.

BOXERS IN THE ADIRONDACKS

Boxing is part of the Adirondack tradition; it has its place in Adirondack history. Boxing began with the travelling boxing bears who entertained early settlers in the Adirondack hamlets and it continued with world champions.

The Adirondacks of the 1920's became *the* place for boxers to train for their fights. The hospitality, the sunshine, the cool nights, and the good food were just what a fighter needed to get into shape. They came and did just that. And America's wealthy crowd followed them.

The Gooley Club camp in Minerva was the first training center for Jimmy Slattery. His Adirondack training paid off when, in 1927, he defeated Slapsie Maxie Rosenbloom to become the world light heavyweight boxing champion. Slattery eventually moved his training center to another better-known location, the Osborne Inn in Speculator where he gained quite a reputation as a beer-drinking brawler. Trouble seemed to follow him around much as it does some of our modern day fighters.

The Town of Benson had its "School of-Boxing." Early in the century, George Swan, who had trained with John L. Sullivan, opened a training center in his old red barn. His students successfully took on all comers until Lysander Call moved in from Lake Pleasant. On election day Lysander took them all on, one by one, including Swan, and defeated each one. He broke the jaw of Oscar Sweet, the last challenger.

Gene Tunney established Speculator's reputation as a prizefighter training center. Tunney became a friend of Bill Osborne during World War I, where he began his boxing career. Bill saw the greatness in Tunney and invited him to train at his hotel after the war. Tunney remembered the offer and when he was to face Jack Dempsey in 1926 he moved to Speculator.

Tunney went on to defeat Dempsey in ten rounds in 1926 and received a controversial decision in the 1927 return bout. He knocked out contender Tom Heeney in 1928 and retired from the ring to get married. During this period, Speculator in the Adirondacks was his legal residence. He attributed his success to daily hikes in the Adirondack woodlands with his guide and friend, "Pants" Lawrence.

The flood of boxers and wealthy fans to the Adirondacks began. Billy Wallace trained for his 1927 fight against Kip Kaplan. Swedish boxer Knute Hansen followed. Maxie Rosenbloom decided to try Speculator. Charlie Bellinger trained at Speculator to fight Lou Scoza. Max Schmeling chose the Adirondacks in 1932 to get ready for Mickey Walker and stayed several years. George Brescia and brothers, Buddy and Max Baer prepared in Adirondack country. The Associated Press reported that Speculator never produced a loser until Max Baer came up against Joe Louis.

It appears that boxing in the Adirondacks began with the bears and ended with the Baers. There are probably many variables which contributed to the demise of prizefight training in the Adirondacks but there is some speculation that, first and foremost, it was Bill Osborne's mother's pies that kept the boxers coming. (I can understand that; I never met a pie I didn't like!) Tunney wrote years later that he "never again tasted anything like them."

Today's pugilists would be wise to look once again to the health-giving features of the Adirondacks where body and mind can be brought to consummation.

PRESIDENTS IN THE ADIRONDACKS

Teddy Roosevelt put the Adirondacks on the map in 1901 by becoming the 26th President of the United States while on a trip to the Tahawus Club in the high peaks of the Adirondacks. It is a well-known Adirondack story and has been well-recorded. Other Presidents had their not-so-well-known Adirondack experiences.

Thomas Jefferson and James Madison vacationed at Lake George before they took the high office. James Monroe and Martin Van Buren did some Adirondack travelling. Chester A. Arthur spent some of his early days in the Adirondacks including sleeping on the pine floor at Moody's, a popular Adirondack hostelry, in 1861. He continued to enjoy the Adirondacks after becoming President in the 1880's.

Paul Smith's 30,000-acre hotel complex near Saranac was the "summer whitehouse" to Presidents. Presidents Grover Cleveland, Benjamin Harrison, Teddy Roosevelt, and Calvin Collidge enjoyed Paul Smith's hospitality. President Coolidge maintained his summer Whitehouse on Osgood Lake. He enjoyed the "magnificent scenery, invigorating air purified by the evergreen forest, pure sparkling water and the opportunity for outdoor diversions." In a Paul Smith's Adirondack Club brochure published in the 1920's by the Troy Times Art Press, President and Mrs. Coolidge are shown with their son, John, and one of their white collies crossing a walking bridge at Paul Smith's. Another photo shows Governor and Mrs. Al Smith, guests of the President. Reportedly, the President enjoyed the fishing from the walking-bridge.

The presidents also found their favorite Adirondack vacation spots throughout the mountains. The Saranac Inn attracted President Grover Cleveland over the years. He also honeymooned there after his White House marriage to Frances Folsom. President Benjamin Harrison eventually built a summer camp on Second Lake in the Fulton Chain near Old Forge. President William McKinley chose Hotel Champlain near Plattsburgh.

The first president that I remember, President Franklin D. Roosevelt, attended the dedication of the Whiteface Mountain Veterans Memorial Highway in 1935. The highway was approved by the New York State Legislature and the voters in 1927 and is one example of the voters' power to amend the "forever wild" Adirondack constitutional protection. The state had wisely purchased 4,500 acres, including some virgin spruce, on Whiteface in 1921. The project was important enough to attract the President. The 8.2-mile toll road in Essex County is still operating today on New York's fifth highest mountain.

When Fort Ticonderoga was restored by the Stephen Pell family in 1908, President William Howard Taft visited the Adirondacks. Another President, George Washington, passed through the Adirondacks on much the same trip to inspect Fort Ticonderoga and Crown Point some 125 years earlier.

When the hostilities ceased in 1783 between Great Britain and the United States, George Washington had some time on his hands. He was waiting for a definitive peace treaty. He wrote to General Philip Schuyler from his Newburgh headquarters, "I have always entertained a great desire to see the northern part of this State." He planned a trip to Lake George, Fort Ticonderoga, and Crown Point. He wrote to the president of Congress a month later telling of his trip as far northward as Crown Point and westward to Fort Stanwix. He was impressed with the "extent and importance" of the vast potential for inland navigation. There is speculation that, in knowing this, Washington attempted an investment in some Adirondack lands.

It appears that our turn-of-the-century presidents knew the value of an Adirondack experience. Today's presidents apparently have missed the sound of a rushing mountain stream, the breathless view from a mountaintop, the dense and quiet woodlands, the shuffling of a wild creature, and the health-giving resources of New York's vast wilderness. Too bad! The positive impact of an Adirondack experience would serve our nation's leaders well.

TEDDY ROOSEVELT—ADIRONDACK PRESIDENT

Teddy Roosevelt, our twenty-sixth president, had his Adirondack connection. He was a well known, devoted outdoorsman. His exploits as a big game hunter and conservationist have been well documented. His Adirondack experiences may not be so well known.

Roosevelt made his mark on the Adirondacks in his early years. His doctor had sent him to the Adirondacks during his youth to improve his health. During his high school and college days he spent the summers in the Adirondacks. He shot his first deer in the Adirondacks.

Roosevelt's quest for knowledge never ceased. He spent his time watching and recording the birdlife of the Adirondacks during these early days. He had done some bird watching in the White Mountains and on Long Island and carried this hobby over to the Adirondack Mountains.

In 1879, while an upperclassman at Harvard, Roosevelt and a friend, H.C. Minot, published a small booklet, "The Summer Birds of the Adirondacks." Their observations of ninety-seven different birds were recorded in August of 1874 and '75 and June 22nd to July 9th, 1877. Roosevelt observed that there were many lakes and a luxuriant forest growth in Franklin County at that time. The deciduous trees were a hundred feet high and the white pines reached a hundred and thirty. He found less birds than in the White Mountains and found that "nests, moreover, seem to be more commonly inaccessible and rarely built beside roads or woodpaths."

Examples of his notes on the birds, each listed with its popular and Latin name, reflect the thoroughness of his study.

Robin- "sometimes found in the woods"

Hermit Thrush- "sings until the middle of August"

Red Crossbill- "the male often sings somewhat like a Purple Finch
     from the top of a tall dead tree"

Swamp Sparrow- "two or three were found in the wet ground, cov-
     ered with very low shrubs, which border the stream
     connecting the Upper Saint Regis and Spitfire Lakes"

Barred Owl- "one shot in August 1875, probably not very rare"

Woodcock- "In July, one was shot at Paul Smiths, none of the in
     habitants knew what it was, or had ever seen
     another"

Loon- "rare, but in 1870 common"

Roosevelt continued his visits to upstate New York after entering political life. He had a close attachment to Gloversville, the Adirondack's gateway city. He was a good friend of Lucius Littauer and stayed often at the Hotel Kingsborough. Teddy Roosevelt continued his attachments to the Adirondacks. He was the only man to become president of the United States while in the Adirondack Mountains of New York. In fact, while Vice President, he was high in the mountains, near Mt. Marcy, when word came that President McKinley was dying.

President McKinley was shot by an anarchist on September 6, 1901 while in Buffalo at the Pan American Exposition. Vice President Roosevelt rushed to Buffalo but was assured by the doctors that McKinley was not critical. Roosevelt left for the Adirondacks to join his family at the Tahawus Club. On September 13, they climbed Mt. Marcy. While eating lunch near Lake Tear-Of-The-Clouds, high point of the Hudson River, guide Harrison Hall arrived with the news that the President had taken a turn for the worse. The fifty-three-year-old Hall had hiked the nine miles up in the rain in just over three hours.

Roosevelt hiked off the mountain to the clubhouse which was ten miles above Tahawus, forty miles from the North Creek Railroad Station. It was getting dark but the Vice President would not wait; he took a lantern and started for North Creek.

Upon seeing Roosevelt's determination, David Hunter hitched up the buckboard and took Roosevelt the ten miles to Tahawus in two hours. Orrin Kellogg drove the next section, nine miles through the darkness to Aiden Lair, in a little over two hours.

A new team with a new driver, Michael Cronin, made the last sixteen miles with his Morgans to North Creek in one hour and forty-one minutes. A record. The Vice President was to catch a special train to Buffalo. It was 5:31 a.m. A telegram waiting at the station informed him that President McKinley had passed away at 2:15 a.m. Roosevelt had become President of the United States in the wilds of the Adirondacks.

Folk history tells of Mike Cronin selling the eight historic horse shoes from his Morgan horses for souvenirs many times over. His daughter, Eloise, has put the story to rest. Her mother told her, "No one ever gave the horse shoes a thought; they were kicked off in the pasture or along the road somewhere. Your father never sold them to anyone." However, the surrey used by Cronin was acquired by the Adirondack Museum in 1968.

XV

Adirondackers Extraordinaire

Seneca Ray Stoddard

EBENEZER EMMONS

To some, "Adirondack" has become such a common part of our vocabulary that we seldom question its origin. Some others may question and speculate on where and how the name originated. The record is clear. The answer can be found in New York State Assembly Document Number 200 of February, 1838.

Until 1838, the Adirondacks had several names. "The Great North Woods" (or Great South Woods if you lived on the St. Lawrence or in Canada) or Northern Wilderness was in common use. "Browns Tract" was accepted by many although it referred to a small region of the mountains. "Couchsuchrage" was used by Native Americans to describe their beaver hunting ground. The early maps referred to New York's wilderness as uninhabited, impassable lands or "The Dismal Wilderness." The explorer John Cabot called it "Prima Vista." France's first name for the Adirondack country was "Avacal" and later "Peruvian." The Dutch called it Hodenosanneega" and later "Corlear Mountains." After the War of 1812 it became "The Macomb Mountains" after General Alexander Macomb. None of these or a dozen other names for the Adirondacks stuck.

Professor Ebenezer Emmons proposed the name that remains with us today. The Professor had been appointed Geologist-in-Chief of the Second District of The Geological Survey of New York. His job was to explore the "mountains of Essex." And this he did. He was among the first to explore Mt. Marcy and to describe the scientific wonder, scenic beauty, and natural resources of the Adirondacks. Our Pacific Coast had been explored before Emmons made his exploration of the Adirondack peaks in 1837.

The trip to Mt. Marcy, at that time called Tahawas or Cloud Splitter by the natives, was commissioned by Governor William Marcy to make a geological survey. The group included the professor from Williams College; James Hall, State Geologist; Professor John Torrey, botanist; Professor C. Redfield, engineer and meteorologist (who wrote an account of the ascent); C.C. Ingham, artist; E. Emmons, Jr.; Archibald MacIntyre and David Henderson, Adirondack landowners; and guides Harry Holt and John Cheney. Sabael's son, Lewis Elijah, guided them part of the way along with two unknown woodsmen (possibly Nicholas Stoner and Captain Gill).

It was not an easy trip. Bushwhacking and animal trails provided the transportation route. The accounts tell of the jungle-like growth of underbrush and the crossing of valleys and ridges of logs, roots, and rocks. Steep climbs and wetlands added to the difficulties. In spite of these challenges of primitive Adirondack country they reached their goal at the top of New York State and the mountains were named with a name that stuck.

Professor Emmons wrote in his report, Assembly Document Number 200: "The cluster of mountains in the neighborhood of the Upper Hudson and Ausable rivers, I propose to call the Adirondack Group, a name by which a well known tribe of Indians who once hunted here may be commemorated." He was referring to the Algonquins who were supposedly called "haderondacks" by the Mohawk Indians. "Hades" means they eat and "garondah" means trees, referring to the Algonquin practice of eating the inner bark of the white pine for Vitamin C.

Professor Emmons, a talented teacher and scientist, went on to other things. He was an accomplished botanist, geologist, mineralogist, and chemist as well as a physician. Some of his geological work became controversial and he was abused by his peers. Later he was proven correct. He followed up his geological survey with a four-year survey of agriculture and then left for a geological survey in North Carolina. He was lost during the Civil War and apparently died in North Carolina sometime in 1863.

Professor Ebenezer Emmons, a man of remarkable gifts, will be remembered in history for his contribution to New York's Great Wilderness. The name, Adirondack, remains a daily reminder of his contribution to the history of one of our nation's greatest regions. Our thanks to Professor Emmons or today we would be trying to pronounce the original official proposed name for the Adirondacks, "The Aganuschionis!"

WILLIAM H. H. MURRAY

Some say that Adirondack Murray's books are unreadable today. Not true. His sentimental fiction weaves tales of the Adirondacks that strike a nerve in today's callous world. They are in demand in the rare bookstores and command a corresponding price.

William Henry Harrison Murray gained his "Adirondack" nickname in 1869 with the publication of a book which "kindled a 1000 campfires." *Adventures in the Wilderness* or *Camp Life in the Adirondacks* was an instant best seller and brought thousands to New York's Great Wilderness. The small book provided a travel description for those who wanted to go to the mountains and a fictional Adirondack story.

Murray was not one who would be expected to write an Adirondack camping book. Murray, not yet thirty, was the pastor of Boston's prestigious Park Street Church. Rising from poor beginnings ("no rich rascals in our family") Murray became a great preacher and was in demand on the lecture circuit. He appeared in the Gloversville Lecture Course in December of 1871. His fee ranged from $100 to $500, a substantial amount in those days.

Murray was an outdoorsman. He said that he had three loves—Old School Theology, the Adirondacks, and horses. He practiced what he preached. One of the many outdoor references in his sermons explained, "The Bible from beginning to end is the work of outdoor men. Go to the seashore, to the mountains, to the wilderness, go anywhere where you can forget your cares and cast aside your burdens."

Murray's trips to the Adirondacks got him in trouble. When he asked for some assistance in his growing ministry at the church some of the congregation responded that he would not need extra help if he spent less time in the woods and with the horses. Murray quit.

Once Murray was separated from the established church he pursued other interests. He formed an independent church, published a religious newspaper, raised horses, lectured, and wrote Adirondack tales. He designed the Murray wagon but over-extended the business and gave his property to his creditors. He failed in the lumber business in Texas. He left his wife. Murray, the great preacher and writer, ended up in Montreal working in an oyster bar.

By 1886, Murray decided to start over. He remarried and moved back to Vermont and continued his lecturing. He wrote the Lake Champlain stories. When finances permitted he rebought his family homestead in Guilford, Connecticut and retired to raise his four daughters. He wrote a book on how he raised four well-mannered, perfect children. I found upon reading it that his secret was isolation. The girls were never exposed to the outside world.

Murray's Adirondack camp life book brought thousand to the Adirondacks when the weather was extra rainy, hotels were not available, and every drunk in town became an Adirondack guide to make a quick buck on the influx. People were consumed by mosquitoes, lost in the woods, and found themselves with poor accommodations. Guidebook writer Stoddard wrote "If Murray's preaching is not a better guide to heaven than his book to the Adirondacks, his congregation might manage to worry through with a cheaper man."

Murray's Adirondack tales are unequalled. His stories of Trapper John Norton were highly popular in their day. A mixture of humor, religion, and the Adirondacks was, and is, one perfect formula for an Adirondack tale. His tales were published and republished in a number of combinations forcing readers to buy each edition in order to get the latest stories. His green cover with the gold illustrations and printing was also repeated over and over with different stories inside.

Murray's writings, slowly dictated to a secretary using a typewriter, included some from outside the Adirondacks. He wrote *The Perfect Horse*, collections of sermons, tales of Texas, the far west, Canada, and Lake Champlain along with the lengthy book on educating his daughters. W.H.H. Murray packed a variety of experiences and tales in his sixty-five years.

Adirondack Murray stands-out as one of the Adirondacks' greatest promoters. He believed that once you enter the Adirondacks, "you can enter upon a voyage the like of which, it is safe to say, the world does not anywhere else furnish." And, we can each take a lesson from his admonition, "Thousands are in Europe today as tourists who never gave a passing thought to this marvelous Adirondack country lying, as it were, at their very door."

VERPLANCK COLVIN

A small news item in the *Little Falls Times* of June 3, 1897 mentions a survey to be made of the Herkimer and Hamilton County line. The line was "desired by the authorities of both counties." Some property owners along the line were escaping taxation because the authorities did not know in what county the land was situated. "Several hotels on the Fulton Chain of Lakes do not pay taxes on this account." Verplanck Colvin, Superintendent of State Land Surveys, was ready to commence work on establishing the line.

Verplanck Colvin was the greatest Adirondacker who ever penetrated that great wilderness. He is the "Father" of the Forest Preserve. He devoted his life to surveying and mapping New York's "crown jewels"—the Adirondacks. For twenty-eight years, 1872-1900, he crossed rivers and lakes, scaled mountains, and traversed the trailless wilderness in all kinds of weather to correct maps, establish lines, determine altitudes, publish reports, and to make recommendations. Much was done on his own time at his own expense.

Colvin was born in 1847 the son of a prominent Albany lawyer and senator. His mother was of the influential Verplanck family of Coeymans. The family gave Verplanck good connections and the opportunity for a good education, including private tutors and Albany Academy. He studied law in the office of Martin Van Buren.

Colvin's stint as a lawyer involved him in land suits and he soon became interested in engineering and surveying. He taught at Hamilton College and the Albany Institute. During his lifetime he served on many boards and in variety of organizations including the American Association for the Advancement of Science, the Appalachian Club of Boston and the Sierra Club. He was the Honorary President of the Adirondack Guides Association.

Colvin went Adirondack camping in 1868. The trip was to Lewey Lake on today's Route 30; it firmed up his lifelong love for the Adirondacks. He climbed Whiteface Mountain the next year. During one of his survey years he visited 250 unexplored Adirondack lakes with guide Mitchell Sabbatis. It would be difficult if not impossible to find someone who spent more time or visited more places in the Adirondacks than Verplanck Colvin.

Colvin began his promotion of preserving the Adirondacks in 1865. He was doing some map work in the Speculator area and in a speech at Lake Pleasant he espoused the creation of an Adirondack Park. Seven years later he was predicting the need for preserving the Adirondack watershed for the downstate cities one hundred years later. (He was right, right to the year). A letter published in the Essex County Republican, December 12, 1882, reemphasized his previous reports on the need for preservation. His survey reports are filled with references to the importance of the Adirondack Preserve.

Verplanck Colvin published eight major reports. His unpublished report of 1898 was published this past year by a group of those who appreciate his work. The reports are unequalled in knowledge or detail. Colvin knew more about the Adirondacks than any who came before or after. Unfortunately, he became discouraged and bitter at the end of his career. The lack of appreciation and support during his lifetime took its toll and he died a broken man.

Colvin once "found" a poem carved on a beech tree near Keene Valley:

> Hundred years ago the Land was rich and strong,
> Political Dishonesty has since made all go wrong,
> 'Tis time to turn the current of the rapid running stream
> And stamp out fraud, corruption, and everything that's mean,
> And One has boldly dared to try
> Him Shall the Nation Ratify!
>
> Woodsman 1876

And "ratify" him they did; during the Centennial of the Adirondack Park suitable plaques were placed on Verplanck Colvin's gravesite in Coeymans and on a selected Adirondack rock in the western Adirondacks. Appropriate ceremonies honored the best friend the Adirondack's ever had—Verplanck Colvin.

ANDREW MOREHOUSE

Andrew Morehouse was a wholesale grocer in New York City with extensive business dealings in many other fields. He had ideas, experience, and some money to invest and made the choice to take a chance on the Adirondack wilderness. He and a couple of partners selected some land around today's Morehouseville and began a boundless journey to success and failure.

Many tried their hand at developing the Adirondack wilderness. It was not easy. Once an investor chose to purchase Adirondack land there was a need for manpower. It took hard work to clear the land for settling. Individuals alone could not survive in the wilderness and the need for an organized group becomes evident. Transportation for people and supplies and, of course, capital were needed in a new Adirondack venture.

Settlers did not come easy. Morehouse found that the shortage of locals willing to go to the Adirondacks led to the recruiting of immigrants. He advertised with circulars, some written in foreign languages. He brought in twenty-four families from France along with twenty-three unnaturalized Germans. He offered the Dutch "land good for farming and raising stock" and "only $1 to $6 acre, easy terms." He showed beechnuts at the docks misrepresenting them as giant buckwheat from the Adirondacks.

Morehouse developed a contract agreement with a time limit on clearing the land and making improvements. The land reverted back to him if the agreement was not completed on time. It turned out to be a bad arrangement.

Andrew Morehouse built an Adirondack home in 1834 and moved with his family to the new land. He began his Adirondack dream in earnest. In many ways he was ahead of his time.

He established the Morehouse Union whereby his settlers owned everything collectively: the land, the buildings, and the products. Young couples and immigrants who lacked capital were able to join. They could work for the Union and acquire credit for needed food and lodging. Morehouse gave a five percent dividend to members who would join for five years and give nine months notice to quit.

Morehouse laid out three objectives for his Union and developed the rules to reach them; to settle and improve wild land, to help each other, and to make others happy. He ruled against alcohol. He set up a court system tolerating no immoral conduct or profanity. The settlement practiced religious freedom and allowed women to own stock and to vote. Members were paid for their time serving in court.

He developed a welfare system and social security to help those unable to work. Those hurt or sick received half-pay during disability. Schools were free but children worked three hours per day.

Morehouse laid out a village and looked forward to a well-defined and profitable community on his Adirondack holdings. An infantry division of the New York Militia was formed in the settlement. The community began to grow and the Town of Morehouse was established by the Legislature in 1835.

Morehouse did not confine himself to a single holding at Morehouseville. He acquired additional lands in the other Adirondack patents totaling some 46,000 acres. He bought some farms in Wells and Lake Pleasant. He laid out the Village of Piseco hoping that it would become the county seat. However, his strict time limits on building and strict "zoning" rules chased settlers away. The settlers came. The land was undeveloped and prosperous farms were off in the future. It was cold and dark and wild in the Adirondacks. Settlers turned around and went back to the city in numbers, some the same day of arrival. The population dropped from two hundred fifty to four during the 1840's. Morehouse pushed for the completion of roads throughout Hamilton County. In 1841 his efforts enticed the Legislature to pass an act for a road from Newkirks Mills to Piseco, a road that still exists today. He worked to get a railroad into his holdings through the southwestern Adirondacks.

The railroad proved to be Morehouse's last hope. When the decision was made in the 1850's not to put a railroad through his southwest holdings at Morehouse and Piseco he was finished. He left his affairs to his son-in-law, Havilla Winchell, and spent his time traveling. He left his wife to seek lodging with friends.

In 1880, seventy-four-year-old Andrew Morehouse was a destitute inmate in the Oneida County Poor House where he eventually passed away. His dream of a populated Adirondack community never reached three hundred and the prosperity he sought remained as elusive as the white-tailed deer who populate the Morehouse forests.

FREDERICK LAW OLMSTED

There are endless stories of "Adirondack Influence" on the lives of people. One such story is the intriguing account of the life of Frederick Law Olmsted. Olmsted, considered to be the founder of American landscape architecture, designed eighty-nine parks in thirty of our states, the United States Capital grounds and the World's Columbian Expo in Chicago, among other well-known accomplishments. The list is endless; how then did the Adirondacks fit into his life?

Frederick Law Olmsted spent his early years in failure, facing trouble finding his way in the world and trying many occupations. He sailed to China, failed at farming, and succeeded for a short time as a journalist while losing money trying to publish. Working for the United States Sanitary Commission and running a mining settlement in California rounded out his early experiences. Apparently, he had a good mind that needed to find the right niche in life.

Frederick had an interest in landscape from his boyhood. He once wrote,"...my pleasure began to be affected by conditions of scenery at an early age." His father took the family on many outings to view the countryside. Frederick read on the subject and visited any park he could find. While others visited great tourist attractions Frederick visited the parks of London, Paris, and Brussels. He wanted such a park for New York City without regard for "...art or fame or money."

The day came. Frederick was having lunch with a friend of his, New York City Park Commissioner Charles Elliott. The commissioner suggested that Frederick apply for the position of Superintendent of Parks. Frederick considered it a challenge and applied. Another friend of his, Washington Irving, was on the board and swung the vote in his favor. He got the job.

The Adirondacks appeared on the scene at this time. New York City was looking for a design for a new park. People were spending Sunday afternoon walking through the cemeteries in order to enjoy the out-of-doors. A park was needed to balance the lives of the thousands who lived in the crowded city.

Frederick looked at the 840-acre space available for a park. It was a discouraging sight. It was filled with squatter's shacks, bone-boiling works, swill-mills, and hog farms. He saw swamps, open sewers, and bramble-covered grounds. He called it, "a pestilential spot, where rank vegetation and miasmatic orders taint every breath of air."

Frederick had great foresight and saw the possibility of creating a great man-made park. He made the determination to design a park so that "the poor of New York City can enjoy what the wealthy enjoy in the Adirondacks." Frederick had visited New York's great wilderness to the north. He saw value in preserving nature for man's enjoyment and use and he wanted to bring it to the people of New York City. He wanted them to have the works of nature in the midst of the works of man.

A $2,000 prize was offered in 1857 for the best design for Central Park. Frederick Law Olmsted joined with architect Calvert Vaux to design the first real park in the United States. They called themselves, "Greenward" and beat the other thirty-three entries.

The designing of Central Park with its hidden roadways and rustic motif led to Olmsted's founding of a landscape architectural firm that lasted in his family for 123 years. His son, Frederick, Jr., was selected as the first head of the professional landscape architecture department at Harvard in 1900. An international organization, the National Association for Olmsted Parks, is dedicated to restoring Olmsted's fame and his parks. Olmsted's home in Boston is now a National Historic Site.

Thus, the Adirondacks influenced Frederick Law Olmsted in the creation of Central Park and beyond. When the call for national parks began in our nation, Frederick was there. He joined the campaign in 1910 and wrote the fundamental statement of purpose for the National Park Service. His love of the out-of-doors and his journalism background produced a statement of purpose for the National Park Act.

"To conserve the scenery and the natural and historic objects and the wildlife therein and to provide for the enjoyment of the same in such manner and by such means as will leave them unimpaired for the enjoyment of future generations." Frederick Law Olmsted and the Adirondacks have made a contribution to each of us and to those who follow; a portion of our natural world will be preserved for generations to come.

DR. EDWARD L. TRUDEAU

Much has been written about the health-giving features of the Adirondacks but none is more dramatic or far-reaching than the research and care-giving of Dr. Edward Livingston Trudeau. His journey to his beloved Adirondacks to die of tuberculosis resulted in the creation of today's Trudeau Institute, a laboratory devoted to biomedical research.

Some hundred years ago little was known about tuberculosis. When E. L. Trudeau's brother contracted the disease he was closed up in an air-tight bedroom to die. Edward faithfully cared for his brother not knowing that, in so doing, the communicable disease would be transmitted to himself. For three months, until his brother died, he spent day and night caring for his every need.

Dr. E. L. Trudeau was born into a family of doctors and seriously studied the profession. He was upset with the unscientific approach to medicine and was predisposed to search for improvements. He was taught that "tuberculosis is a non-contagious, generally incurable disease, due to inherited constitutional peculiarities, perverted humors, and various types of inflammation." His later research took care of these false precepts.

Dr. Trudeau had spent some of his early days in the Adirondacks. When the doctors told him that his health was rapidly deteriorating, he remembered his love "for the great forest and wild life." He journeyed by train and wagon to Paul Smiths Hotel on St. Regis Lake and was carried into his room "weighing no more than a dried lamb-skin!" He came to die yet, with the combination of rest and fresh air, his health improved.

Dr. Trudeau's family joined him in the healthy climate and he stayed the rest of his life. When his strength returned he opened a medical practice for the hotel, guides, and hunting camps. He moved to Saranac Lake, opened the Adirondack Cottage Sanitarium for TB patients and the Saranac Laboratory for the Study of Tuberculosis.

Dr. Trudeau's contacts with the wealthy at Paul Smiths and at his sanitarium made successful fund-raising possible and he "began his lifetime of begging." He raised funds for St. John's in the Wilderness and for the Church of St. Luke the Beloved Physician in Saranac Lake. The Adirondack guides from Paul Smiths Hotel purchased sixteen acres of land on the side of Pisgah Mountain and gave it to Dr. Trudeau for his sanitarium. The fund raising for medical research continues today under the leadership of his grandson, Francis B. Trudeau, Jr. at the Trudeau Institute.

Dr. Trudeau's care of rest and fresh air involved psychological support, health education, and occupational therapy. A trip around Saranac Lake today will reveal the many "cure" cottages with their porches for getting the patients out in the summer and winter air. Thousands of today's North Country residents can trace their families to a Trudeau patient and can attest to the success of his venture.

The Trudeau Sanitarium was closed in 1954 as a result of the effective drug treatment for TB, but some of the buildings have been preserved. They are used for seminars and training sessions by private groups. The new Trudeau Institute opened in 1964 on a different site and is now involved in immune system, cancer, aids, and cell research.

Thus, Dr. Trudeau's love for the Adirondacks founded a pioneer health resort that became an international center for TB cure. His efforts led to boarding cottages, ambulatory cottages, apartments, a sanitarium for foresters, the Will Rogers Sanitarium for movie stars, and an entire town devoted to making people well. Hundreds of doctors have been attracted to the Adirondacks through Dr. Trudeau's efforts. Lives of thousands were changed by the "journey to the Adirondacks to die." The Adirondacks will forever be remembered as the place where, because of Dr. Edward Livingston Trudeau, science and philanthropy came together to help mankind.

JOHN BROWN

We sing about a John Brown who was "a molding in the grave" but which one was it? The Adirondacks embraced two John Browns in its history: John Brown the abolitionist and John Brown the land speculator. Both attempted to tame the Adirondacks in their own way, the first at North Elba and the second near Old Forge.

John Brown of North Elba had a dream. He planned an Adirondack community to provide a home for escaped slaves. He brought his family to Essex County in 1849. Philanthropist Gerritt Smith had offered Adirondack wilderness land to black people who would settle and cultivate it. John Brown made him an offer knowing that it would be a difficult task for black slaves to move north and to farm the land.

Brown proposed, "I will take a farm there myself, clear it and plant it, showing the Negroes how such work should be done. I will also employ some of them on my land, and will look after them in all ways, and will be a kind of father to them." Gerritt Smith agreed.

It was not easy to farm in the remote Adirondacks in the 1800's. Thomas Wentworth Higginson wrote of a trip to John Brown's farm. He described twenty-two miles of mountain road from Keeseville, past wild summits bristling with stumps, through mining villages, to the hamlet of Wilmington with its mountain walls, two miles to the last house, following a mountain stream with a view of Whiteface and finally to the homestead of John Brown. The little frame house, still standing today, was unpainted and surrounded by a clearing.

John Brown had been working to prevent slavery throughout our young country. He heard about the free land in the Adirondacks and how unscrupulous surveyors were cheating the black people who chose to take advantage of Smith's offer. He was a surveyor himself and decided the Adirondacks was a place he could establish a free black community.

John faced too great an obstacle in the Adirondack country of the 1800's. It was a wild place, cold and bleak. It was too cold to raise corn; in the most favorable season they "scarcely grew a few ears for roasting." The stock had to be "wintered" for nearly six months of every year. Winter lasted from November to May. John Brown's black community never reach fruition.

In spite of his hardships John Brown retained his love of the Adirondacks until the end. When facing execution for the fracas at

Harper's Ferry he told his wife, "Mary, I hope you will always live in Essex County." And his burial was arranged in the peaceful mountains.

John Brown of Providence, Rhode Island was born into a wealthy family in 1736. His family founded Brown University and John served as treasurer for many years. In 1772 he led a group in the destruction of a British ship, one of the first blows against the British Crown.

John Brown became a successful merchant, trading with the Far East. He was a friend of George Washington and was active in politics. Somehow his connections caused him to end up with some Adirondack land. Part of the Macomb Purchase had passed to William Constable and then in turn to Samuel Ward, Aaron Burr, James Greenleaf, and to Philip Livingston. From Livingston it was transferred to John Brown for some unknown reason; records were destroyed in a fire at the county clerk's office in Herkimer.

There is some speculation that John Brown's son-in-law, John Francis, won 210,000 acres of Adirondack land in a card game with Burr, Greenleaf, and Livingston while losing $250,000 of Brown's import profit. Brown made his one and only trip to the Adirondack site in 1799 in an effort to recoup his loss.

Brown divided the tract into eight townships. Township Four, originally named "Unanimity" has become today's quadrangle "Number Four." The history of the John Brown Tract is a history of failure. Brown spent large sums of money which were all lost in the wilderness.

The final chapter was tragic. Brown's daughter married Charles Frederick Herreshoff. Herreshoff tried to rebuild the family fortune by developing Brown's Tract. He failed. He shot himself. But that is another story.

NED BUNTLINE

Buffalo Bill died September 19, 1992. He was the last surviving grandchild of famed frontiersman Buffalo Bill Cody. He had legally changed his name to "Buffalo Bill" and was carrying on the Wild West Show promotions of his famous grandfather.

There would have been no Buffalo Bill without Ned Buntline. Many remember Ned as the king of the dime novelists. Others remember him as the man who made Buffalo Bill a national hero. Ned, whose real name was Edward Zane Carroll Judson, was also an Adirondacker.

Ned led an exciting life. He created characters loved by his readers. He ran away to sea, became a decorated naval officer, published two newspapers, wrote a series of dime novels, went bankrupt time and again, and found and promoted Buffalo Bill. He was hung for killing an irate husband, survived the botched-up hanging, and was acquitted by the jury. He was involved in anti-Catholic and anti-British riots. He wrote hymns and, although a drunkard himself, was a sought-after temperance lecturer. It is surprising that the remote and serene Adirondacks appealed to the flamboyant Buntline.

The owner of the *New York Mercury Magazine* encouraged Ned to purchase some Adirondack land. Ned had visited in Eagle Lake country, now Blue Mountain Lake, and settled on a place called "The Eagle's Nest".

Ned's publishers did not count on the problems which arose once Ned took to the mountains. He loved the wilderness and turned to writing poetry. He wrote a dozen lengthy Adirondack poems. The poems were not as profitable as his novels. His publishers made a visit which ended the poem practice and Ned returned to grinding out money-making stories. It earned him some $20,000 per year.

Another Adirondack problem involved Ned's love of the bottle. He had to journey to Glens Falls to mail in his manuscripts. Unfortunately the journey took him past some of his favorite taverns. He stopped at each one along the way and lost two weeks' work on each trip. The publishers got a post office established at Eagle's Nest and Ned became the postmaster. He no longer had an excuse to go to Glens Falls. The move reduced his drinking, although some say that his friend Aaron Sturges smuggled liquor to him from Lake Pleasant.

Ned did not make a good husband. He left his first wife to go to the Adirondacks. He then married his Adirondack housekeeper at Eagle's Nest. She died in childbirth and he went to the city and found another wife. She did not like the Adirondacks. Ned had to hide her shoes so that she couldn't leave him. She eventually went on a visit and never returned. Lonesome Ned gave up on women, and, at the age of forty, joined the Union Army in the Civil War.

Ned's military service was another episode in his controversial career. He became a sergeant, found a way to get into trouble again, and was demoted. Before long he was dishonorably discharged.

Ned, making the best of the situation, took the title of Colonel and went on to new ventures. He found William Cody and put him in a road show that he wrote in four hours. Audiences loved it although most of it was Ned's imagination. Ned and Buffalo Bill soon had a parting of the ways and their partnership was dissolved. Ned settled in Stamford, New York, never to return to his Adirondack cabin.

He had entered the Adirondacks in the 1850's. He hired a guide and taken the old road from Johnstown past Lake Pleasant and around the south shore of Raquette Lake. He loved the Adirondacks. He fished and hunted with his guides. They showed him how to build a bark lean-to in the woods. He learned how to build a campfire and soon adopted the ways of the Adirondackers. In these early years he moved into an old hunter's cabin near the head of the Indian River and lived like a hermit.

Ned's hermit life was ended the night that his cabin burned. He was forced to snowshoe thirty miles to Lake Pleasant. In spite of this set-back, his love of the Adirondacks prevailed and he moved into the cabin at Blue Mountain Lake. He rebuilt this cabin into a gentleman's retreat.

He met others who loved his mountains. Master fisherman Seth Green, later New York State Fish Commissioner, showed Ned how to get the trout.

Ned made friends with Adirondack hermit-guide Alvah Dunning and then started a feud over the hounding of deer. Ned shot one of Alvah's dogs and told him the next bullet was for him. Their feud became well-known but ended when Ned left for the Civil War.

Some of Ned Buntline's best writings were done in the Adirondacks. His Adirondack poetry never gained widespread acceptance, however, it was used extensively in circulars advertising Adirondack summer resorts for over two generations. Ned Buntline, one who lived his life far from the norm and traveled the world, found the Adirondacks: "There is my home—my wildwood home."

A monument to Ned's Adirondack days can be found in the Blue Mountain Lake Cemetery. When his wife died in childbirth at their Adirondack home she and the child were buried under some nearby evergreens. In 1891, the constant desecration of her grave caused millionaire William West Durant to remove the remains to the Blue Mountain Lake Cemetery and to erect a monument to the famous author's family.

JOSEPH BONAPARTE

There is a small lake which lies between the western border of the Blueline and the eastern boundary of Fort Drum. The lake is named Lake Bonaparte. And when we hear Bonaparte we immediately think of Napoleon Bonaparte, Emperor of the French. Most have never heard of his eldest brother, Joseph.

Joseph had an eventful life as head of the Bonaparte family. The father had died and the burden fell on the oldest brother. His ambitious brother, Napoleon, had given him many assignments and, at one point, he turned down the opportunity to become the King of Italy. He became the popular King of Naples in the early 1800's and then switched to become the King of Spain.

When Napoleon met his Waterloo, Joseph decided to escape to America. He arranged the trip and then tried to get his brother Napoleon to go in his place. Joseph envisioned a New France in America. He discussed establishing large manufacturing industries in the Black River Valley to take the business away from England. Napoleon refused to go but had he chosen to come to America we may have had an Adirondack Napoleon story.

Joseph came to America in 1815. He had money, he had been a king, and he was the brother of the most famous man of his day. He was welcomed. He established an estate near Bordentown, New Jersey, where he practiced scientific farming as a country gentleman. He displayed his crown jewels and his famous paintings by DaVinci, Raphael, and Reubens. He wrote to Napoleon offering to join him in captivity, but Napoleon refused the offer.

It was then that Joseph looked to the Adirondack country. He had purchased the land from a speculator, his friend Le Ray de Chaumont, before he came to America. Chaumont owned over 200,000 acres of New York's north country and lived in a chateau on the Black River as early as 1808.

Joseph wanted a hunting ground and found this land on the western slopes of the Adirondack Mountains to his liking. It was a huge tract which he called his "wilderness" and for which he paid $120,000 for 150,000 acres. Eighty cents an acre is a good buy for Adirondack land. Joseph took his friends to his wilderness on hunting expeditions.

In 1822, Joseph decided that he needed a villa in his woods, possibly for his mistress, the daughter of a Philadelphia Quaker family. He built a log fortress on the Blueline at Natural Bridge and a lodge on Lake Bonaparte. The house at Natural Bridge had bullet-proof sleeping rooms. The Bonapartes were in danger until the death of Napoleon.

Joseph divided his time between his New Jersey and Adirondack properties for the next ten years or so, then sold his Adirondack lands to rich merchant John LaFarge, and returned to Europe. He made provisions for his mistress and the daughter she had borne to him. Joseph died in Italy in 1844.

Joseph's daughter, Caroline, ended up teaching language and music in Watertown when her Bonaparte pension ran out. Her husband, who called himself Colonel Benton, was unsuccessful in his money-making schemes including mining on Bonaparte lands and selling some of the woodlands to six different investors. He spent his time imitating Napoleon.

Joseph must have been quite a sight in the Adirondacks. He traveled up the banks of the Hudson and through the Mohawk Valley from New Jersey to get to his Adirondack holdings. He was always accompanied by a large group of friends and attendants. He rode in his coach drawn by six horses through the forest roads. Joseph wore an elegant green hunting suit and made his hunting trips with great pomp and ceremony. He also had a six-oared gondola which he used on the Adirondack waterways much as he did in Italy when he was king. He was well-liked by the neighbors, hunters, and settlers. Joseph of the Adirondacks was probably the closest America came to having a king of its own.

SENECA RAY STODDARD

I do not know how many pictures are taken each year in the Adirondacks but, in my estimation, it is probably one of the most photographed places in the world. And one man probably spent more time and took more Adirondack pictures than one could imagine. (One early 1900's volume alone contained 768 of his photographs.) That man was Seneca Ray Stoddard and he did it in a day when photographic equipment was primitive and cumbersome.

Seneca Ray Stoddard lived during the heydays of the Adirondacks, mid-1800's to the early decades of the 1900's. He was a photographer. He was a writer, editor, and publisher. He was cartographer and an artist. He was an inventor. He was a traveler and a lecturer. And he excelled in each of his pursuits.

Stoddard was known for his publication of Adirondack guidebooks. Although he had written a couple of small illustrated Adirondack books in the early 1870's, he began his successful series of Adirondack guidebooks in 1874 and continued them for the next forty years. He called them *Adirondack Illustrated*. He wrote about the customs, regulations, game laws, train and steamboat schedules, wearing apparel, hotels, inns, restaurants, natural wonders, and the towns and villages of the Adirondacks. His books included everything one would want to know about travel in the Adirondacks. They were well illustrated with his sketches and maps. Reprints are available today.

Stoddard also published a small monthly magazine called *Stoddard's Northern Monthly*. It gave him an opportunity to gather and preserve the stories of the Adirondacks as well as the opportunity to editorialize on the protection of the forests. He sold the magazine along with all of his other books, photographs, and maps from a little storefront in Glens Falls.

Stoddard's photos of the Adirondacks are in great demand today. They claim high prices when they turn up in the flea markets and antique stores. The stereographs made of Stoddard photos are the highest priced wherever they are found. Several years ago a set of Stoddard photos was purchased by a library for over $50,000.

Seneca Ray traveled and photographed around the world but, to me, his best work was done in the Adirondacks. He recorded the guides, tourists, stage coaches, steamboats, hunting parties, fishermen, survey parties, loggers, hotels, camps, and natural vistas on film for posterity. His works are still illustrating books and magazines today. The detail and quality in his photographs make each of them a history lesson in itself.

Stoddard did us all a favor. His work and indirect promotion became a major force in the successful efforts to establish the Forest Preserve in 1885 and the Adirondack Park in 1892. He raised the awareness of the glorious Adirondack country which led to their protection and enjoyment by the generations to come.

Stoddard did his work with a large, old-fashioned camera and tripod using glass plates and emulsions. He hired guides to help carry the bulky cameras, heavy boxes of wet plates, and bottles of chemicals. He took night pictures with burning magnesium metal. He invented a combination photographic plate and film holder. With this invention he could pack fourteen plates or two dozen films in a three-inch space. He also made other improvements to the cameras he used as well as patenting a new, improved electric trolley.

It is hard to imagine the Adirondacks without Seneca Ray Stoddard. His pictures have brought the colorful Adirondack past to the present generation. At one of Stoddards Adirondack lectures in Albany in 1892 it was reported, "Long before eight o'clock every available seat was taken and many were left standing." Should Seneca Ray Stoddard reappear today I am certain that "many would be left standing" again.

HARRY RADFORD

Most have heard of Adirondack Murray, but not too many have heard of Adirondack Harry. Harry was a victim of life's strange twists— the kind of twists that change the course of a life on this unfair earth. Harry planned a tour as an understudy with nationally-famous Murray which was cancelled when Murray was taken sick. And, added to this unfortunate turn of events, Harry, who was a true friend of the wilderness guides throughout his life, was killed by his native guides while on an international hunting trip.

Harry Radford was William Henry Harrison Murray's biographer, and after Murray's demise was the chief promoter of the Adirondack Murray Memorial Association. He wanted to perpetuate Murray's memory, to erect a suitable monument at his grave, preserve Murray's homestead, to support Murray's family, to continue the education of Murray's daughters and to promote Murray's many Adirondack books. His efforts met with little success.

Early in the century, Murray and Radford had planned to take a tour of the Adirondacks and then tour the state campaigning for the Adirondack Park and Adirondack Forest Preserve. They also planned to publish a literary Adirondack magazine. Unfortunately, Murray was taken sick and passed away in 1904 without taking his final tour with Radford.

Harry Radford came close to being another Murray. He shared the same love of the woods and the sharing of the outdoors through the printed word. He was a graduate civil engineer but had begun publishing a small magazine in 1898 when he was eighteen years old called

Woods and Water, devoted to Adirondack information. It was always successful, climbing to over 20,000 subscribers.

Harry became a good friend of the Adirondack guides through his magazine. He supported what the guides' supported and they liked him and his magazine. Harry joined their associations and was usually a speaker at their banquets. He looked after the guides when they came to New York City for the sportsmen shows. In a speech to the Brown's Tract Guides Association in 1903 at Old Forge, Harry described the guide-sport relationship: "The sportsman's relation to his guide is scarcely less close, scarcely less sacred than that of a child to mother."

Harry was persistent in getting good writers for his magazine. He took up causes and persisted until he got results. He fought for the restoration of the moose in the Adirondacks and organized the "Association for Restoring Moose to the Adirondacks" in 1900. His pressure got the bill through the legislature in 1901 and $5,000 was appropriated to release some moose in the Adirondacks. Three were released in 1902 and later another twelve were released without any success.

Harry campaigned for bringing back the elk, caribou, and beaver. William Whitney released twenty-two elk and they were so tame they rapidly disappeared. Harry got bills to restore the bear and beaver passed in 1904 and helped out with some game protection around the country.

Harry extended his writing to other magazines including *Field and Stream*. His influence on Adirondack affairs has never been equaled. He became a noted authority on the Adirondacks. In June of 1900 he appealed to the legislature in his "National Sportsman Magazine's Notes": "We would like to see our Adirondack State Park take a more substantial form than a mere blue boundary line on a green Forest Commission map. Why can't the work be pushed a little faster?"

When Harry's mother died around 1906, Harry ended his magazine career and took up the journeys he had always wanted to do. He became a big game hunter in the Pacific Northwest and Labrador. He arranged to explore Hudson Bay and into the Arctic Circle. He donated some of his mounted game to the major museums.

Harry made his biggest trip in 1910. He was joined by another explorer, Thomas George Street, and they reached the Canadian wilderness in early 1911, never to return. The eventual story which came back to civilization was that the two men were killed by the spears of Eskimo guides over some apparent misunderstanding caused by the language barrier. It is ironic that Adirondack Harry, friend of the guides, ended his days at the hands of those he had protected over the years.

NESSMUK

It is hard to believe that Nessmuk was an Adirondacker. He was born in Massachusetts and died in Pennsylvania. He sailed on a whaling ship out of Cape Cod to the South Pacific in 1840. He was a sergeant in the Civil War. In 1866 he explored the Amazon Valley in Brazil. Later he bushwhacked through the swampy, insect-swarming, malaria laden, little-known Florida. He lived with the Indians and trappers in Ontario, Minnesota, Wisconsin, and Michigan. He became the "law and prophet" of woodcraft and was "the greatest woodsman who ever wrote for *Forest and Stream.*" And he was an Adirondacker.

George Washington Sears, who selected the pen name "Nessmuk" from his Indian guide, was born in 1821 and never began his writing career until 1860, when he was thirty-nine years old. He became a writer for *Porter's Spirit of the Times.* The Civil War ended that career and he wrote some poems for literary magazines and edited a weekly newspaper for a year in 1871.

Nessmuk made his big comeback in his final years with his Adirondack writings. In the 1880's he wrote for *Forest and Stream.* The small one hundred twelve-pound woodsman and his mini-canoes became a national novelty. His Adirondack writings gained widespread recognition that has lasted to this day.

Nessmuk joined that illustrious group of Adirondackers who moved New Yorkers to save the Adirondacks. His writings, added to Colvin's, Stoddard's, Hammond's, and others, became part of the total persuasive piece that became the "forever wild" Adirondacks.

Nessmuk cursed the selfish policy of damming Adirondack waters and the cutting of the giant sawlogs; he accurately predicted over one hundred years ago the devastation of our natural resources. His first-hand experiences with the Adirondacks convinced him that mankind was on the wrong road in the treatment of the earth.

Nessmuk's ten and a half-pound canoe, *The Sairy Gamp*, is in the Adirondack Museum. It was one of three of his lightweight Rushton canoes which made him famous. He took three trips into the Adirondacks and published eighteen articles describing these cruises.

Nessmuk's first canoe, *The Nessmuk*, weighed about eighteen pounds. He used it on his 1880 trip. The second, *Susann Nipper*, weighing sixteen pounds nine ounces, served the second trip a year later. He was too sick to take an 1882 trip but was able to make an 1883 trip in *The Sairy Gamp*. He later took some Florida canoe trips in *The Rushton*, named after the builder, which weighed a little under ten pounds.

Rushton promoted travelling light in the wilderness. He invented an eighteen-ounce double-bitted pocket hatchet which would chop down a ten-inch tree within three minutes. His own small stature called for keeping his load light.

When Nessmuk observed the changes in the Adirondack lakes brought on by the dams, logging, and the tanning industry, he became a pioneer conservationist. He wrote articles to make the public aware and joined in the lawsuits against the tannery owners. He learned early to hate the greed and hypocrisy associated with wealth and became a social reformer.

It was easy for Nessmuk to turn to the wilderness; he was a social dropout. He avoided marriage until he was thirty-five and then had three children. He sometimes worked as a cobbler, his father's trade. Family responsibilities were not in his thinking and he often left the family for the mountains where he socialized with the Adirondack guides. His brother watched over his family.

It was too bad that Nessmuk did not begin his Adirondack writings until he was fifty-eight. His health was failing and he was plagued with his chronic asthma on his canoe trips. He complained of coughing all night and having night sweats. He had planned to cover a thousand miles of Adirondack waters but had to shorten his trips to 206 miles.

George Washington Sears, Nessmuk, ended his days in 1890 with fever, chills, and incessant coughing, and with his debts piling up from his failed ventures. His fame and possible fortune came after his death and continues to this day. His writings are still being published and his name lives on in the annals of Adirondack history.

XVI

Adirondack Hermits and Guides

"French Louie" Seymour

HERMITS

It was not uncommon growing up in an Adirondack village to see a bewhiskered, shabby, sometimes smelly, old man walking into town. Sometimes he was draped with furs and usually had some kind of pack or burlap bag. He was quickly identified as the "resident" hermit at that settlement. Never to be feared, we usually followed him around town. Unfortunately, we never learned his name or talked with him about his past or life in the woods. Well-known Adirondacks hermits French Louie and Noah Rondeau have been immortalized in books, but other communities had lesser known hermits.

Caroga hermit Albert Eschler performed odd jobs for summer residents. Pearley Howard lived alone, although at one time he advertised for a wife. Tip Bowler, Daddy Boynton, and Jeff Reed lived hermit-style lives near Pine Lake and Canada Lake.

Sacandaga Park hermit, Stewart Wilson, made his living by taking tin-type pictures of people sitting on a rustic bench in front of his shack. Benson hermit Daniel Wadsworth supported himself by making shingles. He "squatted" back in the mountains west of Benson for many years and called himself a guide. The state kicked him off the state lands and he moved to Silver Lake where he died at the age of ninety.

Archie "Bobcat" Ranney, believed to be a retired printer, lived as a hermit near Bakers Mills. He was known for his ability to kill and to cook porcupines. I wish I had his recipe. Ebenezer Bowen lived as a hermit near Long Lake during the last half of the 1800's. He called one of his Methodist friends to his deathbed to tell him he was still not a believer. David Smith lived for fifteen years as a hermit on Smiths Lake, now Lake Lila, before he left for the west in disgust over the growing population.

Lake George had a hermit called Indian Charlie. Charlie lived on one of the remote mountains obsessed with hunting panthers. No one knows if he got one. Willard Letson lived in his hermit's cabin on Gilman Lake near Wells. He was killed in a lovers' triangle.

David "Foxey" Brown was purported to have come to the Adirondacks to escape the law for beating a man in Boston. He lived near Lake Pleasant until a tree fell on him and ended his work as a lumberman. He moved to Fall Stream six miles back from Piseco. Visitors were not welcomed by Foxey and he often shot at the game warden, Charlie Preston. Later they became friends.

The superintendent of the Cayautta Division of the FJ and G Railroad, Carlton Banker, became a friend of Foxey, who served as his guide for hunting. Mr. Banker gave Foxey clothes and started a bank account for him. Banker was lost while hunting in 1916 and many thought Foxey had killed him. Foxey could not stand the pressure and left for the south. Banker's body was found in the woods six years later three miles from Piseco.

Alvah Dunning was a well-known hermit of the central Adirondacks. He did not like neighbors, moving from Arietta to Lewey Lake, to Blue Mountain Lake, where he fought with writer Ned Buntline, to Raquette Lake, to Eighth Lake, and to Long Lake to get away from civilization. At one point he moved to the Rocky Mountains to get away from neighbors. He did not like the west and moved back to the Adirondacks.

Alvah Dunning, the man who avoided civilization, met a tragic end. He attended a sportsman show and stopped to spend the night in a Utica Hotel. Upon retiring he blew out the gas lights without turning off the gas. He was found dead in bed in the morning in a gas-filled room.

Adirondack hermits shared much in common. They had a reason for living in solitude in the woods and that reason was strong enough to overcome any fear they may have harbored of cold, hunger, fatigue, or of becoming hurt while alone in the woods. Most could withstand severe cold and pain. And they were immune to the friendly pests of the Adirondacks: the punkies, the black flies, deer flies, mosquitoes, yellow jackets, hornets, house flies, ants, mites, and fleas.

GUIDES

Most old-time Adirondackers will tell you they were born deep in the Adirondack Mountains in a log cabin they built themselves—almost true.

The early settlers in the "Great North Woods" cleared the forests, built a cabin, and settled down to farm. Farming in the foreboding wilderness did not turn out as expected. The soil which grew the giant pines and maples did not produce giant corn and pumpkins. The rocks and climate worked against them.

There was a report that in one Adirondack hamlet they were forced to keep one ten-dollar bill at the general store and pass it around among those who needed it. Thus, the farmers turned to new occupations.

Out of the need to make a living in the wilderness, a new and hardy breed of man appeared—the Adirondack Guide. One early guide, Nick Stoner, could "kindle a fire, climb a tree, cook a dinner, shoot a deer, hook a trout, or scent an animal quicker than any other man." Guides made a good living showing the greenhorn sports, artists, writers, and tourists the wonders and bounty of their Adirondack "territories."

The early guides made $2.50 to $3.00 per day with fifty cents extra if they supplied the boat. They were required to furnish the axe, cooking utensils, and tents. They carried all of the luggage over the carries, although some of the better sports assisted them. The guide cooked the meals and took care of the domestic duties of the camp. And they found the fish, game, and the trail. On top of all of this an early editorial reported that the guides "will work for the laws that keep the forest intact and will protect the fish in our streams and game in our woods." It was not an easy job.

Adirondack guides fell into several categories. There were the unostentatious, introverted guides who worked with quiet, courteous efficiency in the woods. They said little and made that little go a long way.

Other guides were full of remarkable stories and experiences. They never talked unless they were alone or with somebody. Sam, the oldest guide on the Fulton Chain, had only one fault, "his tongue never stops."

The best Adirondack guides were the regular, independent guides whose reputations got them all the work they could handle. Once in the woods they became the boss over their employers and provided a safe and successful trip.

Other guides attached themselves to hotels as hotel guides. Their allegiance was to the hotel owners who paid them and not to the party. Some noted that hanging around in daily proximity to the hotel bar was "very liable to beget that greatest of all vices in a guide—drunkenness!"

The original Adirondack guides were described by the early writers as "like a good wife, indispensable to one's success, pleasure and peace," as "necessary as sugar in tea," as "willing, cheerful, a good cook and strong as an ox," and as "knowing every foot of pathless forest, all woodcraft and all signs of the weather." Guide book writer E.R. Wallace warned against penetrating these wilds unaccompanied by a guide.

Today's Adirondack guides are following in the boot tracks of their colorful predecessors. Licensed by the state, they follow the same goals as Alvah Dunning, Old Mountain Phelps, Mitchell Sabattis, Paul Smith, John Cheney, Sabael Benedict, and others. Today, much as yesteryears, promoting and facilitating travel in the Adirondack wilderness by a competent and reliable guide assures the tourist and sportsman of a safe and successful wilderness experience.

SO YOU WANT TO BE AN ADIRONDACK GUIDE

There are many great recorded stories of the old-time Adirondack guide yet we sometimes fail to record the present. Guides, although at onetime an "endangered species," are alive and well in today's Adirondacks. New regulations are in place to guarantee the public "reliable and competent guides" when penetrating the Adirondack wilds. New history is being created as many are rediscovering the out-of-doors.

New York State began the volunteer registering of guides in 1918. Rugged independent men of the woods who had been guiding for half a century did not take to signing up with Albany. Mandatory licensing began in 1923. Within ten years almost one thousand guides were registered for forest preserve lands. They were given a badge and the power of game protectors.

The 1930's saw the heydays of the guides and the '40's saw their descent. Game protector status was withdrawn in 1944. The number of guides dropped to a handful. World War II veterans, new equipment, and faster transportation to the woods eliminated the need for a guide. The charters of the original guides' associations were withdrawn. Guides were virtually extirpated in New York State.

In the '80's a resurgence occurred. New interest in the out-of-doors and an expansion of outdoor interests led to the increased demand for guides. On March 15, 1983 the New York State Outdoor Guides Association was incorporated. I had written a letter to Wildlife Biologist Mark Brown of the Department of Environmental Conservation early in 1979 suggesting a reorganization of the Adirondack Guides Association.

At the same time other guides were getting concerned about insurance, a clearing house, and upgrading the guiding profession. Joe Hackett, a fulltime guide in the upper Adirondacks, joined with Mark Brown to bring the guides together for a weekend in the spring of 1982. The meeting was held at the Lake Placid Club Resort in cooperation with the Department of Environmental Conservation. A full meeting of the charter members of the new organization was called on December 4, 1982 at the Fulton-Montgomery Community College. Over one hundred guides spent the day discussing and approving the bylaws and code of ethics for the Association. Officers were elected and I began my service as the charter president of the New York State Outdoor Guides Association. (Some of the best people I know are outdoor guides and my association with them is a highpoint of my life.)

The Association was incorporated in February of 1983 and the guides moved ahead with upgrading the profession. New licensing regulations were pursued and the new licensing began in 1985 after two years of cooperative efforts between the NYSOGA, the DEC, and the Legislature. The old guide regulations had been watered down to the point where two dollars would buy a guide's badge whether the applicant had ever been in the woods or not and/or whether he or she was the proper age. Over a thousand people held these licenses and the public could not be sure who could guide them in safety.

Today's guides are licensed in six categories: camping, hiking, whitewater, climbing, hunting, and fishing. There is a general test and a detailed test for each category. Applicants take the tests in their chosen areas. The first license costs $100 for five years and $20 for each additional category with a $200 limit. First aid, water safety if boats are used, and CPR are required of all applicants and all must pass a physical exam. Prospective guides must be legal residents of New York State and at least eighteen years of age. It is not as easy to become a guide today as it was in years gone by.

Today's guides are full-time and part-time. They come from all walks of life. They are male and female. A list or information on becoming a guide can be obtained from NYS Department of Environmental Conservation, Room 408, 50 Wolf Road, Albany, NY 12233-0001. A list of working guides and information on joining the NYS Outdoor Guides Association can be obtained from NYSOGA, Box 915, Saranac Lake, NY 12983.

Some say that the more things change the more they stay the same. Today's guides still show the way, assist with the gear, row the boat, cook the grub, prepare the camp, find the fish and game, and provide clients with a successful Adirondack experience. Guides still hold rendezvous and banquets, care for each other, and provide the public with "competent and reliable guides" as they have for the past hundred years.

THE BROWN'S TRACT GUIDES' ASSOCIATION

The well-known Adirondack Guides Association celebrated its 100th anniversary in 1991. Another, lesser-known guides' association, the short-lived Brown's Tract Guides' Association, was formed seven years after the original group. An increase of guiding in the central Adirondack region caused thirteen experienced guides to gather at Dwight Grant's Boonville boat shop in March of 1898 to organize a new association for guides serving in the Brown's Tract region. Although disbanded within fifteen years, they achieved their lofty goal of creating a more wholesome appreciation of the Adirondacks.

Highly visible and well-attended social events are usually not connected with the rugged outdoor men of a guides' association, yet the Brown's Tract Guides' annual "Guides Banquet" became the social event of the year. Scheduled in February of each year in Old Forge, Inlet, or Boonville it attracted guests from far and wide. The growing Association had opened its membership to associate members which attracted sportsmen who frequented the region along with Adirondack natives other than guides. Associate members outnumbered the guides in the group. Women were allowed to join and to attend the banquet. All had a personal interest in the central Adirondacks. They came together at the annual event to enjoy banqueting, speechmaking, and dancing.

The Brown's Tract Guides' Association proposed objects similar to the Adirondack Guides Association. They pledged themselves to better enforcement of game laws, to work on legislation, to provide "competent and reliable guides" and to maintain uniform wages (four dollars a day).

The Brown's Tract Guides maintained a high level of interest in conservation. When the beaver were wiped out in the Adirondacks at the turn of the century they successfully restocked the forest with them. They personally cared for seven beaver brought from Canada during the winter of 1904. They restocked twenty-five others brought in from

Yellowstone Park in 1906.

Governor Theodore Roosevelt admired the guides and invited seven of them to represent the Association in Albany on legislative matters. Through their efforts the forest was protected, the guides became enforcement officers in the woods, and legislation designed to protect does and fawns and to set shorter seasons for other game was enacted. They opposed jacking deer at night and hunting deer with dogs. They declared open season on any dog chasing deer and kept an annual record of the number of lawless dogs killed by guides.

The guides favored the adding of forested tracts to the state-owned Preserve and opposed lumbering on state lands. They brought the collective experience of their accurate working knowledge to Adirondack affairs and their voices were heard.

The records of the Brown's Tract Guides' Association report that they worked to restore the moose to the Adirondacks. Harry Radford, editor of *Woods and Water* magazine, launched a campaign to get legislative support for a "moose bill." He enlisted the aid of the Brown's Tract guides and in 1901, $5,000 was appropriated. A bull, a cow and a calf were obtained from Canada in 1902 and placed under the watchful eye of Game Protector Ned Ball, a Brown's Tract guide. Although somewhat tame, the moose eventually took to the woods. Four others were added during the summer. The experiment ended in failure, however; within two years they were all shot by hunters.

An attempt by the Brown's Tract guides to stock wapiti, an elk-like animal, in the Adirondacks also failed. Five of the animals were given to the guides by the City of Binghamton. Released in March of 1902 they roamed the forest around the Fulton Chain but refused to "go native." They preferred to look for hand-outs from the households in the hamlets and thus became tame. By fall they were found dead in the woods supposedly shot by a disgruntled hunter.

The Brown's Tract Guides' Association met the fate they tried to prevent in the forest animals. They became an "endangered" species in the Adirondacks. The public acceptance of a clearly defined policy of conservation in the Adirondacks, an acceptance of game laws, and a lessening of the need for a guide in the woods led to the discontinuance of the organized existence of the Brown's Tract Guides' Association. They organized, made their mark on the history of the Adirondacks, and left us with a legacy and our thanks for their contribution to the Adirondacks we enjoy today.

NICHOLAS STONER

Organized guiding in New York State is over one hundred years old. A labor-intensive occupation, which grew out of a need, remains much the same as when the first guide took a greenhorn into the wilderness. Carrying the gear, preparing the grub, and showing the way in the woods remain the major reasons for hiring a wilderness guide. And today's guides look to those who came before for inspiration, stories, and expertise in the Adirondack wilds.

One of the Adirondacks' earliest guides could "kindle a fire, climb a tree, cook a dinner, shoot a deer, hook a trout, or scent an animal quicker than any other man." That guide was Nicholas Stoner. Nick was guiding in the lower Adirondack region long before guiding became a regular profession. He took the hunting, fishing, and surveying parties into the woods from the end of the Revolution to his later years in the 1840's.

Nicholas Stoner served in both major wars of his time. He had grown up on the Fulton County frontier (then Tryon County) and gained an independence in tune with the wilderness. He joined the Revolution at the age of fourteen and served well for six years. When the War of 1812 broke out he re-enlisted to beat the British again, gaining the rank of Major. His military-experience, along with his accomplishments as a deputy sheriff, school trustee, highway superintendent, assessor, hunter, and trapper made him a legend in his own time. Jeptha Simms wrote about Nick in the 1850's and had the local folk hero verify the stories.

Nick knew the importance of his firearm to life in the woods. It served him well on many occasions, including an experience where he shot into a bear's mouth to free his dog. His rifle was made by William Avery in Salisbury and cost over $70. It was worth it. A similar rifle was used by his sometimes wilderness partner, Nat Foster.

Nick's rifle had a single barrel with two locks, one set so that the upper charge of powder rested upon the lower bullet. The locks were made for percussion pills. It was better than the average gun. Nick carved his name in the stock; there would never be any doubt about ownership. The whereabouts of his rifle is one of today's Adirondack mysteries.

Nick's companions in the woods shared his love of the Adirondacks. Captain Gill, a Native American who lived in a wigwam at the

Lake Pleasant outlet, was a good friend of the Stoners. Many thought Nick to be an "Indian Hater." It was not true. Nick only "hated" the Indians who killed his father and those who interfered with his livelihood by stealing from his traps.

Captain Gill and Nick became well-known trappers for setting records at Richard Dodge's Astor Fur Trading Post in Johnstown. Captain Gill delighted in telling the story of Nick and a friend, Obadiah Wilkins, fishing up in Bleecker. While Nick was at the camp preparing a meal, some Indians approached his fishing partner on one of the Sacandaga tributaries. While trying to run him off the Indians asked if he had a partner. Obadiah responded, "Yes, at camp, Nick Stoner." With the sound of this famous name, the Indians were heard crashing through the underbrush in search of new hunting grounds.

Nick spent his final years at Newkirks Mills near Caroga Lake. He supplemented his small pension with his earnings as an Adirondack guide. He assisted Lawrence Vrooman in laying out a road from north of the Mohawk River into Piseco country through the Oxbow Tract.

It was on one of these surveying trips that Nick revealed his proficiency as a guide. Nick, the patriot, who usually found himself leading the Fourth-of-July parade in Gloversville and Johnstown, found himself back in the mountains on the day of celebration.

Nick found some ice in the rocks on the side of one of the mountains, and, marking the spot with the American Flag he always carried in his packbasket, he hiked to Piseco Lake. He captured a large turtle on the beach and took 172 eggs from it. Returning to his ice cache, he made chilled eggnog for the surveying party and served it up with turtle soup. Thus, one of the Adirondack's first guides was able to celebrate the Fourth-of-July in New York's great wilderness.

JOHN CHENEY

Too bad that John Cheney, early nineteenth century Adirondack guide, did not have a good biographer like Nick Stoner, Nat Foster, French Louie, and Noah Rondeau did. He was an adventurous Adirondack original who played a major role in opening up the far wilderness of the Great North Woods. His name appears in some of the earliest accounts of the Adirondacks by writers such as S. R. Stoddard, Charles Lanman, Charles Fenno Hoffman, and J. T. Headley.

I once thought that I would learn something new about "The Mighty Hunter," John Cheney. An 1853 musical composition by Williams Purves entitled "The Adirondac Deer Hunt Galop" was dedicated to John Cheney. Apparently Purves had met Cheney or read about him in Hoffman's 1839 *Wild Life of the Forest* book. Most Adirondack folk songs have a dozen or so verses and I assumed "The Adirondac Deer Hunt Galop" would be the same. After much searching I located a copy in the Library of Congress, paid $19, and waited a year to get it. Unfortunately, the joke was on me, it was seven pages of musical composition and no words!

John Cheney made a name for himself while employed by the Adirondack Iron Works near Tahawus. He was involved in an unfortunate accident where one of the owners, David Henderson, was killed by a pistol that Cheney had left cocked (subject of another column). Cheney also was one of the first guides up Mt. Marcy, guiding Professor Emmons in 1837. He was referred to as "The Indian Guide" on that trip.

It is believed that John Cheney was born in New Hampshire around 1800 and moved with his family to Ticonderoga. When he was thirty he decided that Ticonderoga was getting too crowded. John preferred the woods so he took his dog and left for the remote Essex County wilderness. He found a home in the woods and stayed for the rest of his life.

John Cheney was a tough Adirondacker. He armed himself with a custom-made, eleven-inch pistol (which he gave to the Albany museum) and a jackknife and survived the hardships and dangers of the woods. He once shot an attacking panther and, in another episode, shot his own foot, clubbed a deer for food, made rustic crutches, and hiked fourteen miles out of the wilderness. The wound laid him up for six months.

Cheney was in charge of supplying the iron works with fish and game. In a thirteen year period he accounted for six hundred deer, four hundred sable, nineteen moose, forty-eight bears, seven wild cats, six wolves, thirty otter, a panther, and a beaver. Little wonder that he gained the title of "The Mighty Hunter."

The Adirondack Iron Works Company gave Cheney a farm on the road to Schroon Lake. He married a Newcomb girl and had two sons. In 1874, one of his sons went insane, shot his seventy-four-year-old father in the face and burned their house down. Cheney passed away three years later.

John Cheney, the Mighty Hunter, was described by those who knew him as "small, slight of stature," "gentle, unassuming in manners," "mild and pleasant," and a "lover of nature and solitude." Hardly what his title might lead one to believe but his inner strength and sturdy character gave him the "strength and agility of the tiger" when roused. Adirondack guide, John Cheney, was a true man of the mountains.

ALVAH DUNNING

Alvah Dunning had a hero. His hero was Nicholas Stoner, Revolutionary War hero, scout and guide, who claimed today's Fulton and Hamilton Counties as his territory. Alvah's father, "Scout Dunning," was a good friend of Nick Stoner and the young Alvah learned everything that he could about the remarkable Nick. He could tell many a tale about his hero.

Alvah followed in Nick's footsteps. He became a lover of the Adirondack wilderness. His father settled at Lake Pleasant in the early 1800's and Alvah began hunting and trapping at the age of six. He guided the first white men into Raquette Lake country when he was twelve.

Alvah killed his first moose at the age of eleven. His shot was so accurate, having gone through the ear into the animal's brain, that no bullet hole could be found in the hide. His father teased him, "You only scart him to death." Alvah and his father later specialized in getting moose, killing and selling three or four in one day. The moose were plentiful until the winter of 1854-55 when they disappeared from the Adirondacks, supposedly from a brainworm infection.

Alvah had trouble with an unfaithful wife in his early forties, left the Lake Pleasant-Piseco Lake country, and took to the deeper woods where he sought solitude most of his adult life. He had no need for friends and did not welcome neighbors. He worked as a guide but said, "I'd rather they'd stay ter hum and keep their money. They're mostly durned fools, anyhow!" Alvah had little use for city folk who believed that the earth was round! He died believing that the earth was flat and stationary. Alvah would tip over his coffee cup and dump the coffee out, logically explaining that that is what would happen if the city folk were right.

Alvah also had trouble believing that there was a need for game laws. His family had lived off the woods. There was plenty of game in the woods and it was there to feed him when he was hungry. He felt that they were saving the game for "them city dwellers with velvet suits and pop-guns, that can't hit a deer if they see it, and don't want it if they do hit it!" Alvah only killed game when he needed it and, out of respect for the old hunter's conservation beliefs, the authorities never arrested him.

Alvah made one of his many moves to Blue Mountain Lake to seek solitude. He met his neighbor, writer Ned Buntline, who had discovered and promoted Buffalo Bill. Alvah became Ned's guide and helper. They quickly became enemies when Ned promoted the game laws which Alvah detested. Ned could buy his supplies; Alvah had to hunt and fish for his. They argued and then erupted into a full-fledged guerrilla feud. Alvah left for the solitude of Raquette Lake.

Alvah enjoyed Raquette Lake for twelve years, living on an island during the later years. He met the preacher/writer Adirondack W.H.H. Murray, whom he liked. Murray appreciated those who worked as Adirondack guides. He reported, "A skillful active well-mannered guide is a joy and consolation, a source of constant pleasure to the whole party."

Alvah was "forced" to leave Raquette Lake by the Durants and then took to the shores of Eighth Lake. He spent the next few years moving back and forth from Raquette to Eighth Lake looking for complete solitude. When he heard that a train was coming he decided, with a tear in his eye, that "I guess I've lived too long." The eighty-three-year-old woodsman left for the Rocky Mountains.

Alvah missed the Adirondacks; he was back in less than a year. He settled on Raquette Lake, reluctantly giving up some of his hermit ways. He spent his later winters with his sister in Syracuse.

Alvah's tragic death was an irony of fate. Civilization was his enemy and he met his death by one of civilization's inventions. Returning from a sportsman show he spent the night in a Utica hotel. He blew out the gas jets upon retiring only to be asphyxiated by the leaking gas during the night.

ORSON SCHOFIELD PHELPS—
"OLD MOUNTAIN" PHELPS

Those who learned to live off the bounty of the Adirondack wilderness were ofttimes misunderstood by others. "Shiftless," "lazy trapper," "slack provider," and "irresponsible" were the terms used to describe those who spent their waking hours in the woods. Some said that they "couldn't hold a job." Add to this the thought that they were unclean and possibly bug infected and you can see why they bordered on being social outcasts.

The granddaddy of Adirondack "social outcasts" was Orson Schofield Phelps—Old Mountain Phelps of Keene Valley. His thrifty, hardworking neighbors considered him lazy and accused him often of idleness. Phelps had no use for soap, never took a bath, saying, "I don't believe in that etarnal sozzlin'." He bragged that no water had struck his back for forty years. Old Phelps lived to be eighty-eight; cleanliness, or the lack thereof, apparently has little affect on longevity.

Old Mountain Phelps had arrived in the Adirondacks from Vermont in 1830. His father came to survey some land and Orson tagged along. He loved the mountains and got a job at the MacIntyre mine. He left the mine when owner David Henderson was killed and settled in Keene Valley. Melinda Lamb became his wife and he settled down in the land he loved.

Phelps' neighbors were prosperous farmers and stood in sharp contrast to the one who loved the woods and mountains. Phelps loved nature and according to Adirondack historian, Alfred Donaldson, had a "poetic cast of thought." He did some writing for the *Essex County Republican* newspaper which revealed his genius. One of the tragedies of history is that Old Mountain Phelps was not "discovered" by a publisher who would have encouraged his writings. We lost the Adirondack "Burroughs" or "Thoreau."

Old Mountain Phelps loved to climb Mt. Marcy. He called it Mt. Mercy or My Mercy. He blazed the first trail in 1849 and made the ascent over a hundred times. He took the first two women up the mountain in 1850.

On one occasion, Phelps took a group of young ladies to the top of "Mercy." They giggled and chattered all the way up and, once on the summit, proceeded to talk of clothes and fashions. The old guide, who considered the mountain sacred and the view bordering on a religious experience, was furious. "They may have passed many dangerous spots on the way up", he raved, "but they were in the greatest danger on the top. I had half a mind ter kick the silly things off my mountain!"

Phelps was a primitive philosopher and counted many of the intellects of his day as friends. He considered his time in the mountains and his friendship with men of real intellect worth more than all the money the world could give him.

Old Mountain Phelps coined his own words. The feeling he experienced on the top of Marcy was "heaven up-h'isted-ness." When he was asked to guide someone up the mountain he responded with "I caller-late I kin do it." He called a hike on a trail a "reg'lar walk" and a trip through the wilds a "random scoot." When the going got tough it became a "reg'lar random scoot of a rigmarole!"

Old Mountain Phelps was the fortunate one. He learned to love the mountains. He saw what others did not see. He understood what others missed. His passionate love of the forest and mountains made him the real proprietor of the Adirondacks. He wrote:

> "Fresh from their creator they have all come to me And I must soon leave to unborn generations those scenes that so long have been dear to my sight who will hereafter view them with varied emotions, and volumes about the great Adirondacks will write."

LOUIS SEYMOUR— "FRENCH LOUIE"

The old guide entered the rustic camp with his usual grin and twinkling eyes. The big buck downed that day made his party happy. He had dressed it out, carried it to the hanging rack behind the house, and was ready to cook up some fried potatoes and squash and a few slabs of venison.

The hunter-turned-cook took down his big cast iron frying pan hanging beside the old cook stove, scraped out the residue from the previous meal and began to cut up his fare for a tasty evening meal.

"Aren't you going to wash before you do that?" one of his city-bred hunters asked in a commanding fashion.

Louie, for it was French Louie the hermit guide, grinned again. "Heck no, by jo, I never wash during the hunting season, the deer would scent me a mile away!"

Louie had his own rules and ran a tight ship. His two-story cabin beyond Perkins Clearing, halfway between Newtons Corners (Speculator) and Indian Lake in the West Canada Lakes country was a favorite spot for hunters, especially couples. Louie insisted that the girls always slept upstairs and the boys downstairs in front of the fireplace. He made the beds of balsam boughs for four or five couples at any one time. He never allowed drinking in the woods, although he made up for it when he made his twice yearly trip to Speculator.

French Louie was a French Canadian, Louis Seymour, who arrived in the Adirondacks about 1869. He joined the lumber operation at Griffin and built himself a cabin at Lewey Lake. Another hermit, Sam Seymour, moved in across the lake and claimed to be related to Louie. The independent Louie did not like this so he moved on to the West Canada Lakes. He lived in the woods for over thirty years, from the 1870's until 1915.

There are many stories about French Louie and most of them are in a book written by Harvey Dunham in 1953 and reprinted many times since then. It is one of the best Adirondack books ever written containing pictures and stories not found in the general literature.

The Whitman Journals contain a reference to French Louie's troubles with the law. They did not bother him too much but at times were forced to arrest him for taking deer out of season. He would show up in Speculator with a hundred deer hides on his sled. It was difficult to get a conviction of Louie because most of the "locals" were in sympathy with Louie or believed that "Hamilton County was left out of the state game regulations." When Oliver Whitman served on the jury in 1895 he recorded, "The jurey brought in no cose of action in favor of Seymour."

Louie planned a trip to Speculator each March to sell his winter's take of pelts. When he reached the top of Page Hill he would let out a series of piercing, wild animal cries that would bring the village children running. They loved Louie. He liked kids, not adults, and he would give them nickels or candy. He entertained them with imitations of the Adirondack animals. Time meant nothing to this Adirondack hermit and, unfortunately for the residents of Speculator, he would sometimes arrive in the middle of the night with his wild animal sounds.

Louie spent a bundle on each trip to the Speculator hotels and bars and although all were happy to see him come, they were also happy to see him go. Boat builder, blacksmith John F. Buyce served as his banker and saved much of his money for him.

His last trip was a tragedy. He felt a pain in his side in the winter of 1915. He caught a few trout through the ice and snowshoed to his Pillsbury Camp, about halfway to the Speculator road. The next day he went on to Speculator to get a room at Brooks Hotel. He was sicker in the evening and Ernie and Nora Brooks called the doctor. Octogenarian Louie passed away before morning; the Gloversville newspaper reported that he died of Bright's Disease.

Louie was given a "decent" funeral in the Speculator Methodist church. The Town of Arietta joined with the Town of Lake Pleasant to contribute $76.90 toward burial expenses. The local school was closed for the funeral. The children who loved him so well filed past the casket placing a balsam sprig in it and then lined the street to the cemetery with balsam and pine branches. He is buried in the Speculator cemetery where a permanent tombstone was donated in 1954 with pennies collected by the school children.

A more appropriate monument to Louie can be found in the West Canada Lake country. His fireplace, laid up with great effort in his later years, was left standing when his cabin was removed from the "forever wild" Adirondacks.

NOAH JOHN RONDEAU

Noah John Rondeau spent 381 continuous days in the Adirondacks from May first of 1943 to May 16,1944. He had begun his Adirondack Cold River hermitage in 1902, made seasonal visits for many years and by 1929 was spending winter and summer in the wilderness. In 1940, he spent the entire year alone with the exception of ten days. Noah was a true Adirondack hermit.

Noah lived in the heart of Essex County High Peak country. He called his isolated settlement, Cold River City (population 1). The 5'2" Noah built a low-ceilinged 8'x10' cabin on a high bluff over the Cold River Flow. (His cabin is in the Adirondack Museum today.) It was ten miles northeast of Long Lake Village. A trip to Noah's place required a nineteen-mile hike or an over-twelve-mile canoe trek from any direction. Noah did not have too many visitors.

Noah was a rebellious teenager. At fifteen, he ran away from home. He hated his father and said that he "wished he'd shot him." Noah was one of nine children in a religious family. His brothers and sisters considered him disrespectful. Noah had his own strong opinions, recording in his journals, "I left my father Peter Rondeau, his stick, his abuse of me, his religion, his Priest, and his fool God."

It appears that Noah was highly intelligent but only stayed in school long enough to complete eighth grade. He worked as a barber, a carpenter, and a mason. He was not cut out for common labor and, saying to himself, "What care I?" took to the woods.

Fortunately, Noah met Dan Emmett, a Native American, who taught him hunting, fishing, trapping, and how to make baskets, balsam pillows, canoes, and bows and arrows. He taught Noah the ways of the woods, thus enabling Noah to survive in the years to come.

Noah settled on lands owned by the Santa Clara Lumber Company in order to avoid additional confrontations with the state. He had enough trouble violating game regulations. He built his two small cabins, one the "Town Hall" and the other, the guest room, the "Hall of Records." Noah surrounded his settlement with twelve-foot-high teepees which provided additional living quarters and a source of winter wood. You might say that he lived in his own woodpile. He notched each stick at stove lengths and broke them off in the winter time when he needed wood for his stove. He kept his fire going for 138 continuous days during one bad winter.

Noah took his library with him to the woods. He had sixty books including astronomy, science, philosophy, the classics such as Thoreau, and the Bible. He was well-read and an avid scholar of the stars. Noah was also an accomplished violinist and held regular evening concerts attended by the Adirondack deer.

The old hermit, Noah Rondeau, became a legend in his own time. Beginning in 1947 he made public appearances at sportsman shows, sponsored by his former enemy, the New York State Conservation Department. With his long white beard he served as Santa Claus at the North Pole resort for a period of time. He became an honorary member of the Troy Forty-Sixers, the mountain climbing club. I saw him at the Amsterdam Sportsman Show in 1947 where visitors were throwing dollar bills into his old Adirondack packbasket.

Sixty-seven-year-old Noah left his Adirondack sanctuary for the last time in 1950. The big blow-down had made the woods unsafe and the authorities asked him to move out. He moved in with relatives in Saranac Lake where he passed away in August of 1967 at the age of eighty-four. He is buried in the North Elba Cemetery.

One of Noah John Rondeau's last correspondences written in April of his final year reflects his conversion and the wisdom that he gained during his years in the cathedral of the Adirondacks:

"And now closing: In spite of my sickness and weakness; I have certain facts to think about that make me so happy—I could cry and laugh at the same time; and I pray Jehovah, God Almighty; and his Son, Jesus Christ, that they will so bless you and yours that you will escape the plagues to come; and be ready for God's Kingdom which is near at hand. Noah John Rondeau."

FRANK A. LAWRENCE— "PANTS" LAWRENCE

In our family, clothes were passed down from older children to the younger children until they fell apart. It was true of most of the Adirondack families. In fact, in some cases, we could not wait to grow into a favorite shirt or pair of overalls and rolled them up to fit. And such is the story of "Pants" Lawrence.

Frank A. Lawrence, number one guide when New York State decided to license guides in 1918, was at the bottom of the line in the Lawrence family. He inherited the pants, not only from his four older brothers, but from his father as well. They did not always fit too well and he soon received the nickname of "Pants."

Frank's nickname served him well over the years. He was a sociable guide and "Pants" made him unique. When he ran for sheriff of Hamilton County in 1906 his campaign included a card with a pair of pants on the clothesline with the words. "VOTE FOR PANTS." It worked; he was elected.

Pants Lawrence typifies the Adirondacker. He loved the wilderness, was good at making use of its resources, and made good use of the humor and stories associated with life in the foreboding wilds. Accepting what life gave him and adapting to the times in which he lived made him an Adirondacker worth knowing.

Pants' father, Peter, moved into the Adirondacks with one of the early waves of settlers in 1846. Peter taught his five sons the ways of the woods. They became Adirondack guides. They were good hunters. They ran a hunting camp at Pillsbury Lake. And Frank became well-known for preserving the Adirondack traditions.

Pants had the physical characteristics of a great Adirondack guide. He grew (and outgrew the pants!) to six feet three inches tall, was well built, and had a booming voice. People naturally listened to him.

Pants always said that he was not a drinker; he limited himself to enough to float a ship. When he got older he gave up because the "ships were getting bigger and bigger."

Pants was a storyteller and originated many of the stories passed down today, including the common story using the theme of a snake biting wood and making it swell to several times its size. Pants would point out where it was used.

Pants became his own worst enemy when he told the town clerk's wife that he was not a full-fledged guide. "I take ladies up the river to pick flowers, you might say that I am a pond-lily guide," he told her. From that day on he was called the "Pond-lily Guide," even though he did not really appreciate it.

Pants operated the Adirondack Inn at Wells at one time. He also helped to promote his brother-in-law Lee Fountain's business at White-house near Wells. He pasted molasses on the sides of the notch at Mud Lake to slow down the winter winds and to get them stuck. In the sum-mer they cut them out with a cross-cut saw and put them in the ice house to be used to cool the dining room at the Whitehouse. It was well-known for its cool dining room before the age of air-conditioning and Pants' story helped to explain it.

Pants guided championship boxer Gene Tunney when he trained at Speculator. They were good friends and Gene helped to pay Pants' bills when he was forced in his late sixties to enter a nursing home in Gloversville. Gene also gave him assistance when Pants was sent to Utica, where he eventually passed away. Gene and his friends wanted to bury Pants in his beloved Adirondacks, but his second wife refused and his is buried on Utica Hospital grounds.

It is ironic that Pants' good friend, Broadway star Emily Stevens, was also denied her chance to be buried in the Adirondacks. She had left a message for Pants to take care of her burial but it was found in her apartment too late to be honored. Pants always said it was the great-est regret of his life, little knowing that it would also happen to him.

PAUL SMITH

The Adirondack region is a land of people—people who can do many things. Its history is filled with those who were caterers and guides. Lumbermen played their roles. Merchants and real estate developers made their marks. Road builders and railroad builders penetrated the wilderness. Telegraph, telephone, and electric companies followed the settlements. Remote post offices employed postmasters. And there was one man in the Adirondacks who was all of the above and more— Paul Smith. Paul combined his vision with effective action and became the number one Adirondack entrepreneur of all time.

Paul Smith of the Adirondacks did not begin his life as Paul or in the Adirondacks. Apollos Smith began his life in Vermont, where he found work on a Lake Champlain supply boat while still a teenager. During the slow season the captain of the boat took Pol (later became Paul) to the Adirondacks. He was a quick learner and soon became an expert in finding the fish and game.

Paul decided to become a wilderness guide. Two dollars a day was good money for doing what he enjoyed the most. By the time that he was twenty-three, in 1848, he opened a "sporting house" in Franklin County and hired his mother and father to assist him. By 1851 he saved enough to buy two hundred acres on the Saranac River and to build Hunter's Home for ten men. Room and board was $1.25 a day. The menu included fresh trout, venison, ham, and partridge.

The sports liked Paul Smith's place and wanted to bring their families for vacation. Ten years after opening his first venture Paul purchased fifty acres on St. Regis Lake for $6.00 per acre. With backing from his wealthy clients he built a giant hotel which grew to ten times his previous place.

Paul worked on the construction of his new hotel during the winter. At the same time he hiked twenty miles on snowshoes each weekend to Franklin Falls to court Lydia Martin. It was his good fortune. Emma Willard-educated Lydia became the backbone of the hotel business. They married in 1859 when Paul was thirty-four.

Paul formed the Paul Smith Hotel Company with his wife and three sons, Henry, Phelps, and Apollos, Jr.. He expanded to 30,000 acres which included ten lakes. His enterprise included the building of an electric company which took in Lake Placid, Saranac Lake, and the surrounding area. His electric railroad ran the seven miles to Lake Clear to connect with the Pullman cars from New York City. He opened a store, operated a sixty-horse stable, a four-story warehouse, boathouse, laundry, sawmill, a casino with a bowling alley, pool room, grill, and kitchen. He employed over fifty guides. He also sold real estate and was postmaster for his own Paul Smith post office.

The Paul Smith Hotel attracted the rich and famous. President-Grover Cleveland enjoyed the hospitality. W. H. Harrison, Teddy Roosevelt, and Calvin Coolidge found Paul Smith's in the Adirondacks. P. T. Barnum spent his vacations there. Millionaires E. H. Harriman, the Vanderbilts, and the Rockefellers stayed at Paul Smith's. Dr. Livingston Trudeau, TB pioneer, considered Paul Smith's Hotel the best spot in the world.

Paul died at the age of eighty-seven in 1912 and his son Phelps kept the hotel going until his death in 1937. He willed the wealth and properties to establish a coed, non-sectarian college of arts and science in his father's memory. The present-day college specializes in liberal arts, forestry, and hotel management. Paul Smith pioneered the Adirondack resort industry and it lives on today in one of our state's finest colleges.

CHARLIE REESE

Charlie Reese was a great friend; he always had time to tell me about the Adirondacks. I was in my teens working as a store boy in Mosher's Northville general store. Charlie made a weekly trip from Wells to lay in his supplies. Tall and lanky with only a slight stoop of age, his natural, brushcut-style hair remained its natural brownish color all of his life. We speculated that it was because he continued to tramp the three or four miles up the east side of those Adirondack Mountains to dig gingshang (ginseng).

Charlie weathered the storms of life in the Adirondacks along with the climax maple trees which surrounded his small cottage in the lowlands. His wrinkled features told a story of coping with the wilderness much as the wrinkled bark of the maple tells a story. Charlie could change his wrinkled brow from the deep contemplation of pensive thought to the dancing, twinkling lines of mirth when a favorite story sprung from his memory bank.

Charlie had two favorite sayings: "...in my estimation, in my estimation..." and "that's just the way it was in the Adirondacks." The first introduced his philosophy or belief and the second added credibility to his firsthand account of life in the Adirondacks. He held strong opinions on many Adirondack subjects including "what happened to the trout?" and "where are the deer?"

Charlie had his own way of trapping his listener by setting the story with a puzzling statement such as " I don't know where the deer all is." He then proceeded to continue the suspense for another forty-five minutes weaving a tale that led up to an explanation.

Charlie's stories would go like this:

"Let me tell you about trout fishing. Now years ago when you were going in you didn't take a pole. You took a line and hook and cut an alder after you got there, you know, one bout the right size for fishin. . . . especially this time of year, right now, go in there. Now you wouldn't have a basket; you had a syrup can, a gallon syrup can, this is the way it was in the Adirondacks, just the way I'm tellin' it. You had a rope around it and you put it right around your middle like this, and you'd fill that syrup can with trout—native trout!

We did it many times. Go in on a Saturday night, me and my cousin, Ernie Hitchcock, to an old hunting camp. Must of been there since 1912, no, 1918; well, from the time I was ten to eighteen, I guess. This hunting camp had everything. It had a kitchen and everything. We'd go in, you know he was younger than I was, and kill eight or ten hedgehogs. The camp had a cook stove, a big old cook stove.

I don't know how that woodchuck got in there! You know that reservoir on the end of the stove where they heated water; how the devil he got in there I don't know. We built up a fire and we heard something. We heard a scratching sound in the stove. I opened the cover and that damn woodchuck jumped right out.

You know, we'd kill eight or ten hedgehogs every time, or maybe five or six, something like that. Well, anyway, we'd go in there to fish below the Second Pond Flow in the rough water. It wasn't nothing to get twenty-five to thirty trout or all you could eat. You could always buy one from George Diefendorf on the hill. He lived on the hill where you go in and he caught 'em by the half a dishpan full.

Whenever you walked along that stream you'd see a fawn deer. You would see these little fawn on an island in the stream the reason that they could see what was coming and they could get into the water quick if anything takes after 'em. I was in there once with Ad Farr and her husband and brother and she picked up a fawn and patted him. You know, she could hardly get away from that fawn; you see, he tried to follow her wherever she went."

Charlie had many tales to tell. His some forty years as an Adirondack guide supplied him with a lifetime of experiences. Some of his stories included tales of fox hunting, the fisher influence on the deer herd, how to "ketch" hedgehogs, haying the Adirondack way and gingshang hunting. His stories tell of one man's relationship with the Adirondacks; tales that demonstrate once again that man can live in harmony with the land he loves.

UNKNOWN ADIRONDACK GUIDES

There are some famous and some not-so-famous Adirondack guides. We know about Paul Smith, Old Mountain Phelps, French Louie, John Cheney, Alvah Dunning, John Plumley, Nick Stoner, Oliver Whitman, and Charlie Reese because someone took the time and effort to write about them. When Frederick Leach wrote his article on Nick Stoner for the April, 1965, *American Heritage Magazine* he observed: "To become a successful local hero, get a good biographer and outlive your detractors". Too bad some of the lesser-known Adirondack guides did not find a good biographer.

I would like to know more about some of the Adirondacks' "unknown" guides. We know a little about some of the early mountain guides because they appeared on postcards around the turn of the century. There is one card with a beardless guide carrying a packbasket and a fishpole with the caption "Sam Barton, a noted Adirondack Guide." Another card shows a full white bearded guide with the notation, "Sam – the oldest guide on the chain." Mart Moody, "Famous Guide of Tupper Lake" appears on another card. Other postcards have surfaced which show unnamed guides in guideboats and at Adirondack camps.

Some of the old Adirondack guides appeared briefly in the magazines of their day. A 1912 issue of *Forest and Stream* used Adirondack photos to illustrate an article on a guide up in Maine. One of the photos is a close-up of an old guide sitting on a log with his rifle. The caption gives a brief biography, "Uncle Tom Solomon, the grand old man of Dun Brook, Eagle River, Rock River, and Beaver River. Famous as an Adirondack Guide in late forties up to 1895. Born 1825; died 1911."

Another photo in the 1912 *Forest and Stream* shows "Dick Bird now at Indian Lake, a famous Adirondack guide in late forties and up to ten years ago. Still does a little trapping. Born about 1828." He was sitting on the same log used in the other photo and holding what appears to be the same rifle. It may indicate that the two old guides were posing for a professional photographer.

Some guides live in the memories of those who knew them. There are those who remember Bill Glassbrook at Forked Lake. Some still know or have mentioned Bill Courtney, a Piseco Lake guide, Tony Deepe of North River, Lester Dunham of Wells, Marvin Pedrick of Piseco, Skunk Griffis of Gloversviile, Matthew Beach of Long Lake, John K. Brown of Elizabethtown, William Robison of Lewey Lake, and Loren Kelly of Oppenheim. There was Ed Arnold on the Fulton Chain, Harvey Moody and Sam Dunning in Saranac country, Bill Nye in North Elba, Dick Crego in the Browns Tract, and Philo Scott at Cranberry Creek. And the list goes on.

Adirondack guides came from all walks of life. There were teacher guides, doctor guides, lumberjack guides, businessmen guides, and farmer guides. There were Native American guides and black guides. There were hermit guides and female guides. And in some cases, children who were growing up in the Adirondack wilds served as very capable guides for city folk.

Guides were rugged and independent but they believed in joining together to help each other. (Although one old guide was heard to say that he would not join any organization that would have someone like himself as a member!) The Adirondack Guides Association and the Browns Tract Guides Association were the two major groups. Warren Slater, P.A. Soloman and Alonzo Dudley of Saranac Lake and Thomas Redwood of Paul Smiths were officers in the Adirondack Guides Association. A. G. Delmarsh and Fred Burke were officers of the Brown Tract Guides. Each association had well over a hundred members at any one time.

It would have a made a great story to have the Adirondack experiences of all of these guides put down in print. Their stories would fill volumes. All we can hope is that those who remember will share their stories and get them written down for those who appreciate the history and lore of New York's great Adirondack country.

[*Publisher's Note:* Since this column was written, North Country Books, Inc. published a comprehensive history of the Adirondack guides. *Guides of the Adirondacks: A History* by Charles Brumley, was published in 1994 and is still in print.]

XVII

Adirondack Hotels, Ranches, Resorts, Clubs, and Camps

WHITEHOUSE

A chimney stands in the wilderness. It is all that is left of the "Whitehouse" in the Adirondacks. The "Whitehouse" was once a thriving resort on the Northville-Lake Placid Trail. A trip up the West Hill road behind Lake Algonquin at Wells and "nine miles over dirt road through the woods" took you to Lee Fountain's Whitehouse.

No one knows when it was first called the Whitehouse. The name has been traced back as far as 1899. The construction of the road has been traced to Civil War times and there were two owners of the property before Lee Fountain. The Whitehouse history goes back a long time.

The Whitehouse was a large, white farmhouse. Lee Fountain operated a lodge and cabin business at the site during the early 1900's. It was rumored that politicians from Albany would travel to this remote Adirondack wilderness resort to make their major political decisions.

The main lodge, the Whitehouse, contained a 22'x30' dining hall which seated forty and a 12'x22' lounge and a 8'x12' living room for guests. The water supply was gravity fed from a cool mountain spring.

The Whitehouse kitchen had two six-hole ranges and a large ice-box. It connected to a walk-in cooler and an icehouse. The lodge contained six bedrooms.

The complex included a summer cottage and four cabins. A boys' camp with five sleeping buildings for fifty boys was added to the enterprise. The camp included 22'x50' mess hall and a 30'x30' recreation hall. The chimney of the recreation hall still stands at the end of the cable bridge built in 1962 by Ranger Lou Simons and three local men over the Sacandaga River.

Many Adirondack sportsmen remember the hospitality at the Whitehouse. It was not uncommon to fish or hunt in the West Hill country and stop at the Whitehouse to be treated to a full course dinner of venison and trout. The Whitehouse gardens provided fresh produce and the heavy-timbered barn housed a herd of dairy cows.

Guests were attracted to the Whitehouse from all over the state. The property included three hundred acres on both sides of the river and provided access to the "entire Adirondack mountains including the trails, the forests, the lakes and the state maintained lean-tos."

The Whitehouse business offered no public telephone and no public electric power. Phone messages were left at Parker's Store in Wells. Kerosene lamps and a Knowlson engine generator provided some light when needed.

The property was purchased by Milo Niffen and Edward Richards and operated as a hunting preserve until the late '50's. It was then purchased by the State of New York for $80 an acre and returned to the wilderness. The buildings were removed and the land became an undeveloped campground for hikers, campers, tourists, Boy Scouts, recreational vehicles, and "wandering litterbugs." Thus, the Adirondack wilderness swallowed up the once-thriving complex.

The Whitehouse is the subject of a folk song by the late song writer Archlus (Pete) Craig of Wells. He reflects the feelings of those who knew the once-existing Whitehouse enterprise.

> "Now it's maintained for the wandering litterbugs;
> the State finally owns the whole tract
> but each time I got to that valley
> I wish for those good old days back."

THE SAGAMORES

Communications in the Adirondacks have always had their barriers. It is hard to know what is happening on the other side of the mountains. Proper names were used and reused. We know that the names Deer Lake, Fawn Lake, Buck Pond, Mud Lake, Lost Pond, Beaver Pond, etc. were duplicated throughout the Adirondack Mountains. We also need to note that Adirondack businesses ran this same risk of duplication of names.

Sagamore was one of these. It came from Native American title for the chief or second in command. In James Fenimore Cooper's *The Last of the Mohicans*, Sagamore was "the oldest and highest in rank." It is a worthy word to name an Adirondack enterprise. It has been used for a lake, hotel, lodges, and camps, some of which remain today.

The most interesting of the Sagamores is known as the Sagamore Lodge near Raquette Lake. It is still in use today and can be enjoyed by all. Site of one of the "Adirondack Great Camps," Sagamore Lodge includes the main lodge and more than fifteen assorted structures. The support buildings; the dormitory, barn, school house, blacksmith shop, coops, carpenter's shop, and wood sheds were saved from demolition by the voters of New York State in 1983.

The log-sided camp was built for $250,000 by William West Durant in 1897. It was used by the Durants and later by the Vanderbilts until 1954. It was then donated to Syracuse University who, in turn, sold it to the National Humanistic Society in 1975 for use as a conference and education center. With the addition of the outbuildings it has become a worthwhile stop for tourists. Educational programs are available throughout the year with participants enjoying lodging and facilities at an Adirondack "Great Camp."

Long Lake had a Sagamore Hotel. It was on a point west of the Route 30 bridge. Mitchell Sabattis had visited the site along with his father, Captain Peter, and another Native American father and son, the Thompsons. Mitchell eventually purchased the land.

During the winter of 1881-82 William Dornburgh purchased the Sagamore site from Mitchell. On May 1, 1882 he began construction of a hotel in partnership with Edmund Butler, Jr. It was completed a year later at a cost of five to seven thousand dollars.

The Long Lake Sagamore was destroyed by fire on Jan 16, 1889. It was rebuilt. Stoddard's 1892 Guidebook contains a full page ad for "The New Sagamore, replacing the house destroyed by fire in 1889." It boasted accommodations for two hundred guests. It was open all year under the proprietorship of E. Butler. It also offered telegraph and daily mail, a real service in the early Adirondacks.

The Long Lake Town Hall was located in the basement of the Sagamore Hotel until 1927. It was the subject of some controversy over the years while providing a steady income for the hotel.

The Long Lake Sagamore was closed and torn down in 1960. It was a fate common to many Adirondack hotels.

Lake George had its Sagamores. An antique brochure advertises "The Sagamore on Lake George." It was owned and operated by T. Edmund Krumholz, who also operated a winter hotel in South Carolina.

The four-story Sagamore Hotel offered bowling, bathing, fishing, sailing, shooting, croquet, tennis, rowing, golf, baseball, music, billards, riding, driving, and a garage. It provided a broad view of Lake George. The "new State road" from Saratoga "will make automobiling very desirable."

The other Lake George Sagamore is still in operation today. The three hundred fifty-room resort is located on Lake George at Bolton Landing. Open all year for vacationers and conferences, the Sagamore Resort offers pools, beach, boats, and tennis along with today's usual hotel amenities. The giant complex has been in operation, off and on, for over forty years. Expansion has made it into the largest of the Adirondack Sagamores.

Thus the Adirondacks had their Sagamores, yet, there was one more duplication worth mentioning. Teddy Roosevelt, who became President of the United States while climbing the Adirondack High Peaks, named his Long Island home "Sagamore Hill."

DUDE RANCHES

They say business is down. Money for conferences is limited. Traditional conference groups have grown beyond the accommodation size of many Adirondack resorts. The days of the Adirondack conference centers are not what they used to be.

The day of the auction was wet and gloomy. The November chill was in the air. It fit the situation. Another once-thriving Adirondack dude ranch/conference center/resort was going to the auction block.

Hidden Valley Ranch had been a prominent resort since 1940. It had evolved from a small dude ranch to a full-fledged conference center with accommodations for over three hundred. It kept up with the times. One family had owned it for the past twenty-seven years. Tennis courts, indoor and outdoor pools, horse and ski trails, a ski tow, a lake, and full eating and sleeping accommodations made Hidden Valley the ideal spot for vacation and conference.

Housing in fifteen rustic log cottages followed the Adirondack camp tradition. The giant, well-caulked logs inside and outside have mellowed to their golden color. The stone fireplaces flash their warm glow across golden rafters. Native stone walls add to the Adirondack ambience both inside and outside the buildings. Well-kept, tree-covered lawns and footpaths connected the cottages. The corral and stables, the lake and ski slope surround the conclave.

The auctioneer came from out of town. The land was sold in eight tracts. The price was by the acre and complicated by a combination bidding procedure. The bidder could bid an acre price and choose from tract two, three, four, or five, or any combination thereof. Phase two bidders could outbid the phase one bidders and take the land away. The phase one bidder could recoup by a five percent overbid. The detailed directions for this Adirondack auction took over half an hour; it was not a simple act to dispose of a $3.2 million Adirondack tract. It was complicated further by the need to avoid selling landlocked tracts.

Tract one contained the conference center. Everything for the dude ranch was on the 110 acres with 1,000 feet of lake frontage on Lake-Vanare. The center was well-developed and there is room for expansion. The Adirondack Park Agency allows a twenty-five percent expansion every five years.

The auction began late and only when a wealthy looking gentleman announced that he had a plane to catch. Good thing that they started, he purchased the entire three hundred-plus acres in phase two of the bidding for a million and a half dollars. Others had bid on individual tracts, following their Adirondack dreams of lake frontage or wilderness acreage, but they were unable to meet the price in the complicated phase two bidding. Phase one had totaled only $552,000.

Hidden Valley is not the only Adirondack dude ranch in Warren County. The Lake Lazerne area had more dude ranches than any other section in the east in the 1940's. At one time Warren County had twenty dude ranches and was known as the "Capital of Dude Ranch Country." *The Adirondack Guide* published by the Adirondack Resorts Press, Inc. of Lake George listed Arehart's Thousand Acres, Northwoods Dude Ranch, Sun Canyon, Jack Murrays, Roaring Brook, Stony Creek, Rocking Ridge Ranch, and Hidden Valley. The Eastern Dude Ranches Association helped to promote the "old west" in the east.

The dude ranches offered horses, canoes, boats, bicycles, swimming, horseshoes, table and regular tennis, badminton, and archery, along with the much sought after Adirondack environment for their guests. Music and rodeos were part of the western offerings. Good food was served ranch style and the season extended from early spring to the late fall. The informality of the dude ranches brought visitors back year after year.

About a half dozen dude ranches still operate in the Adirondacks today. Those in need of rest, recreation, or retreat find them more than adequate. The have come a long way from their early beginnings when horseback riding and western music were the main offerings. Some longtime visitors report that they have spent so much time on the Adirondack dude ranches that "even the horses know us!"

LAKE PISECO TROUT CLUB

Lake Piseco (Piseco Lake) in Hamilton County has its place in Adirondack and American history. It is the site of the first sports club in New York State and possibly our nation.

The year was 1840. America was discovering the out-of-doors. The Great North Woods was becoming a place of recreation and enjoyment instead of a "dismal wilderness." Six gentlemen formed themselves into a fishing club after visiting annually, beginning in 1830, "one of those beautiful sheets of water that abound in Hamilton County." It became the Lake Piseco Trout Club.

The Lake Piseco Trout Club purchased land on Piseco Lake and, at first, built a rude hut made of logs. This led to the purchase of one hundred acres and the erection of a fishing lodge called Walton Hall, named after their "mentor" Izaak Walton. It contained a room for each member and a large hall for activities and equipment.

The Lake Piseco Trout Club was a first class operation. In addition to their accommodations they each had their own boat and oarsman. Each day after breakfast they would troll the lake, passing and repassing each other. They would meet at a common point for lunch. Across the lake from the lodge they had a shanty for use in foul weather and for preparing fish.

The oarsmen used for trolling had to be strong in stature to keep up the pace needed to land the fish. It is assumed they were using some type of guideboats with their long oars and appropriate speeds. Locals of record who worked for the Lake Piseco Trout Club included Amos, Alvah, and Michael Dunning, Floyd F. Lobb, old Eli, Daniel and Henry Rudes, and John Nichols.

The Club kept a journal of the catches. The trout were divided into lake trout and speckled trout. The lake trout had five rows of spots on the side while the speckled had two. The tail of the laker was square and the tail of the speckled was forked. Most of the speckled trout were caught in the lake and the lake trout were caught in the outlet.

The number of trout taken from the lake by the Lake Piseco Trout Club is hard to believe. In one five year period they recorded more than two tons of fish. In nine days of June 1842, they took 629 pounds of trout weighing individually from eight to twelve pounds. One monster trout weighed over twenty-six pounds. In 1844 one member caught forty-four pounds of trout in one day. Other large catches were recorded in the journals until 1851 when a disappointing 109 pounds caused them to disband. Apparently, they had overfished the lake. It was a time in history when nature's bounty was "endless" and there for the taking.

Most of the fishing was done by trolling using "tackle of the most delicate kind; a leader of six to nine feet, of single gut, with snell having five hooks arranged with two at the end placed back to back, two more one inch above, and a fifth, or slip hook, one inch above, which passes through and secures the upper and lower jaw of the minnow serving as bait; one of the middle hooks is placed in the back of the bait, and one of the lower hooks in the tail." Each fisherman used two rods and reels at a time. When a fish struck, the other rod was handed to the oarsman to reel it in to prevent tangling or falling overboard. Fly fishing was used at the outlet although the "moschitos [sic], midges or punkies, and black flies presented a drawback to fishing there."

The members of the club included J. E. Duane, a Scott, George E. Warren, Henry Yail, and the Reverend George W. Bethune. The Reverend Bethune served as the American editor of Izaak Walton's *The Complete Angler*. He included a report of the Lake Piseco Trout Club in the 1880 edition.

The journals of the Lake Piseco Trout Club add to Adirondack history. In 1842 they arrived from Troy, New York City, and Medford, Massachusetts to eat breakfast at Matthew Cheney's in Piseco. They told of dining in 1843 at the new hotel at Lake Pleasant, kept by Ephraim Philips. In 1843 they complained about Lake Pleasant-Piseco road which was bad from continued rain. Several bridges were carried away and they had to ford streams to get to Piseco. They recorded overnight fishing trips to West River where they got "fifty pounds of fish and twice that number of black fly bites." Franciscos Inn in Wells was a favorite dining place for Club members on the way to Piseco.

The somewhat short-lived Lake Piseco Trout Club signaled the beginning of sportsmen finding rest and recreation in the Adirondacks. Other clubs have come and gone but the idea remains today. Thousands of acres of great Adirondack country are owned or leased by clubs organized so that their members can afford and have access to the bounty of the Adirondacks. However, the days of over-fishing have gone; the sportsman's philosophy has changed from taking all nature has to offer to developing programs for restocking, regulations, and self-discipline on the lakes and streams of the Adirondacks.

PRIVATE LAND CLUBS AND
CAMP COOPERATIVES

One of the methods of gaining a piece of the Adirondacks is to find enough friends who share your desire. There is a history in the Adirondacks of those who fell in love with a piece of Adirondack country and joined together to obtain ownership. Some of these early enterprises have survived the recessions, wars, and financial constraints over the years.

The Piseco Company, one hundred years old this year, is one such venture. Albert Doubleday and his college friends loved the Piseco Lake country and invested $745 each to acquire the lands enjoyed by their families for six generations.

The Irondequoit Club Inn, built by the Piseco Company, is located on six hundred acres surrounding Piseco Lake in Hamilton County. The Inn, once used exclusively by members and guests is now open to the public. Tent sites and cabins are also available. Opening to the public is one concession used by the once-private enterprises to meet rising costs of operation.

The Irondequoit Inn is the subject of a new book compiled by members of the Piseco Company who have been tied to the enterprise for many years. *Life at an Adirondack Inn* is a collection of stories and pictures of this Adirondack resort for the past hundred years. Its profusion of family pictures speaks to the emphasis the cooperative camps placed on the value of extended family activities. It is a story of sacrifice and tight financing, love and work, to hold on to a choice piece of Adirondack country. With some families in the third and fourth generation the community has grown from fourteen to over a hundred.

The North Woods Club near Minerva celebrated their one hundredth year in 1986. A small booklet, *The North Woods Club, 1886-1986*, was written by Leila Fosburgh Wilson in honor of the event. It tells a similar tale of those who ventured into the Adirondack wilderness, fell in love with the woods and mountains, and joined together to preserve a piece for family use over the generations.

The North Woods lands originated with a squatter. In 1854 the Reverend Thomas Baker of Chestertown was allowed to log on the lands of Augustus Sherman of Albany. He built a small log house and later replaced it with a three story log rooming house. Visitors came, eventually formed the Adirondack Preserve Association, and bought the 5,000-acre property in 1887. It later became the North Woods Club to avoid confusion with other Adirondack groups.

The North Woods Club attracted some well-to-do and well-known members. Winslow Homer painted most of his Adirondack scenes at the Club. His painting of the two local guides in front of Beaver Mountain is one of the best-known Adirondack paintings. Hugh Fosburgh wrote one of his books, *A Clearing in the Wilderness*, detailing his life at the North Woods Club. Other painters came including John Fitch and Eliphalet Terry. Clayt Seagers became a part of the North Woods painters along with Gary Carson, Margaret Kays, and Marsha Donahue. Alfred Whitney and Andrew Mellon joined the Club when their fishing club near Johnstown, Pennsylvania caused a flood killing 2,000 people.

The North Woods Club charged $30 dues a year and $1.50 day to board at the Club House. Guides charged $2.50 a day. Maids were available for fifteen cents per hour while male labor was twenty-five cents per hour. Members were limited to twenty trout per day and three deer per season. All fish were shared in the common kitchen. By 1890, they had seventy male members and took five hundred trout and just five deer that year. (In 1946 one 520-pound "deer" turned out to be an elk!) Women were rejected for membership until 1912.

The North Woods Club had its ups and downs. It was put up for sale at one point but received no buyers. The war years and the depressions caused a loss in members and in 1940 only four were left. Loyal members held on and revitalized the Club. In 1980 a portion of the property retained as "forever wild" had to be logged to meet expenses. The clubs did what had to be done over the years to hold on to their Adirondack lands.

The development of a water supply and plumbing was always a burden for the clubs. The North Woods Club put in a water closet for the gentlemen in 1911 and another for the employees. (Evidently, "the women were expected to be camels!") A tub and slop sink were located in the Club House and baths cost fifty cents. A wandering cow fell into the septic tank one hot August day and provided some extra activity for a reluctant crew.

The Adirondack League Club on the Hamilton-Herkimer County line near Old Forge celebrated its hundredth year in 1990. The Bisby Club had formed in 1878 under the direction or General R. U. Sherman of Utica and merged with the Adirondack League Club in 1892. Their property extends from Little Moose Lake southeast to West Canada Creek.

The Adirondack League Club was considered the largest proprietary sporting club in the Adirondacks, if not in the world, in the decades after it was formed. They were organized to "preserve and conserve the forest, protect the game and fish, promote scientific forestry, and to maintain a preserve for the benefit of the members." The Club bought 104,000 virgin acres for $475,000 in 1890. Through additional purchases and leases they obtained a total of 200,000 acres.

The Adirondack League Club built their headquarters on Jock's Lake, named after Jonathan Wright, an Adirondack trapper and hunter. They renamed it Honnedaga Lake meaning "clear water." Jock's friend, Nicholas Stoner did not approve of the name change so he named one of the Club's other lakes, Nick's Lake.

The original shares were sold for $1,000 entitling the owner to 1/500 interest, a five acre plot and two hundred feet of waterfront for a private cottage. The club still owns 50,000 acres today and leases an additional 22,000 including fifty-six lakes and ponds. The club, with some three hundred members, is now involved in a landmark case protecting their rights to the Moose River which runs through their property.

The Tahawus Club, located on the old Iron Works property in Tahawus, was first called the Preston Ponds Club in 1876. They leased lands from the Adirondack Iron and Steel Company. In 1877 they leased all of the property and became the Adirondack Club. In 1898 they settled on the name, The Tahawus Club, and leased lands from the McIntyre Iron Company.

The new club limited its membership to twenty with thirty non-voting associate members. They remodeled the old mining boarding house for a clubhouse and constructed a fish hatchery. They limited fishing and purchased a bull and cow moose from Nova Scotia. They remembered that the "mighty hunter," John Cheney, had taken large numbers of moose and felt that they could be easily reintroduced.

The Tahawus Club, like many of the Adirondack clubs, evolved from a sporting club for men into a family club. Teddy Roosevelt became president while on a family visit to the Tahawus Club. New York governors Hughes and Whitman were guests at the Club. Artists including Henry Inman, Charles Ingham, Alexander Wyant, and Thomas Cole enjoyed the Club.

Other cooperative land ventures appeared on the Adirondack scene over the years. They all shared some commonalties. They began with a group of humans who loved a piece of Adirondack country; they had the means to make a purchase; they persisted in devising ways to hold on to the land; and they made the Adirondacks a part of their family life.

CIVILIAN CONSERVATION CORPS CAMPS

Some say that we could use a good Civilian Conservation Corps today. Born in the Great Depression, the CCC camps of yesteryears helped many a family through the hard times and provided a positive experience for our nation's young men. And the Adirondacks reaped the benefits of the labor provided by the CCC camps within her borders.

President Franklin D. Roosevelt proposed the New Deal camps when he was elected and Congress promptly passed them on March 31, 1933. They survived for nine years and provided work for thousands. The workers, mostly from the cities, earned thirty dollars and twenty-five dollars of it was sent home to the family.

The Adirondacks provided a great place for the young men to work. There was an endless list of improvements available in the natural surroundings of the mountains. Work on stream improvements, dams, campsites, trails, weed and pest control, and fire control became a part of the lives of those who had never experienced the out-of-doors. Today's generations are still benefiting from the CCC projects.

By May of 1933, CCC camps were constructed at Arietta, Tupper Lake, Fish Creek Pond, Wawbeek, and Mountain Pond. In 1934 a CCC camp was constructed on the road to Sacandaga Lake near Speculator. It is the site of today's 4-H Camp. Another was constructed at Paul Smiths. Moffits Beach and Golden Beach campsites were developed by the boys from the Adirondack CCC camps.

The CCC camp at Speculator hit the headlines in April of 1989 when a CCC mural on the wall of the 4-H recreation building was moved to the Adirondack Museum in Blue Mountain Lake. Under the donation agreement the mural was replaced in the rec hall by a large size photograph of the mural.

The building and facilities of the CCC camp in Speculator had been presented to the 4-H camp committee in February of 1945, although the land was owned by the Harvey Behlen Estate. It was later purchased by Fred Rulison and leased to the 4-H camp until November, 1967 when they purchased the 4.4 acre plot. The Paul Smiths and Speculator CCC camps had been the last to close in the Adirondacks.

The CCC camps of some two hundred boys were well-organized. The U.S. Army set up and supervised the camps. They were formal and well-disciplined. Reveille and retreat ceremonies were held daily on the parade ground. Communities welcomed the well-behaved boys and fought against the eventual closings. The Hamilton County supervisors passed a resolution commending the CCC for their work in the county "Most marvelous and useful undertaking" at minimal cost. They reported no trouble of any kind for law enforcement.

The projects of the CCC were proposed by the Conservation Department and supervised by the rangers. Local residents called Local Experienced Men (LEM's) provided the technical assistance and a tie to the communities. They also planned field days of swimming, boxing, and other athletic events for the off work hours.

There was some concern about the work of "Roosevelt's Tree Army" in the Adirondacks but it was minimal. The Association for the Protection of the Adirondacks objected to the cutting of fire truck trails but they did not take it to court. They, along with the Adirondack Mountain Club, supported the building of ski trails in the Preserve.

Today the alumni of the CCC camps of the 30's have organized a national organization with headquarters in Falls Church, Virginia. They continue to promote the need for today's youth to be given the same opportunity to improve their minds and bodies as was given to the CCC boys of the 1930's. The Civilian Conservation Corps is a great program and what better place to do it than in the Adirondacks.

ADIRONDACK "GREAT CAMPS"

"Let's go up to camp," has echoed across city homes for over a hundred years. And it means something different to different folk; an Adirondack camp can be everything from a "three-sided shanty" to a remote backcountry bunk-bedded hunting camp. It can also mean a trip to one of the "Great Camps" of the Adirondacks.

Great Camps reflect an attempt by the wealthy to bring a standard of living, normally foreign to the wilderness, to the Adirondacks. Vacationing at a Great Camp created a summer colony that could compete with Newport, Rhode Island, Cape Cod, or Florida. Some also "wintered" in the Adirondacks.

The list of Great Camp owners in the Adirondacks reads like a who's who among the nation's wealthy: Vanderbilt, Durant, Whitney, Garvin, Huntington, Morgan, Post, Rockefeller, and Webb among others. They brought their wealth to the wilderness and employed hundreds to maintain a style of living unequalled in wilderness history.

You can visit a Great Camp today. Sagamore, near Raquette Lake, formerly a Durant/Vanderbilt camp, is owned by the National Humanistic Society and is open to visitors. Pine Knot on a Raquette Lake peninsula, the Huntington camp, is owned by SUNY Cortland and a visit by boat can be arranged. You can hike the some four miles into Camp Santanoni at Newcomb, property of New York State, and formerly owned by the Pruyn family. Camp Topridge (Hutridge), the former Post estate, is no longer open to the public. Other Great Camps are privately owned and, if you move in the right circles, you might get in to see them.

Great Camps share some common characteristics. They are made of native materials, massive field stones, and Adirondack logs. A Great Camp is actually a group of structures, each with a specific purpose. The buildings feature loggins (open arcades), turrets, brackets, mansard roofs, elaborate porches, bay windows, lintels, and oriels (projecting windows). They are decorated with rustic work and furnished with rustic twig furniture.

Some of the Great Camps have up to twenty-five or thirty separate buildings. No one is certain as to why they were designed this way but it evolved from other practices of the day. When the wealthy first came to the Adirondacks they made extensive use of giant wall tents. They had a tent for sleeping, a tent for socializing, a cook's tent, a dining tent, and so on. Some surmise that when they decided to build, this practice was continued. Another reason for the separate building practice is more practical. It was a fire prevention measure. When the cook burned down the kitchen building the rest of the camp was saved. It was easier to fight a fire in one building and save the rest of the camp than it would be if they were all in one giant building. It proved to be true in a fire just a few years ago at Pine Knot. The kitchen building burned but the rest of the camp was saved.

One name rises above all others when it comes to Great Camp builders. William West Durant, son of the railroad Durants who built the Atlantic to Pacific railroad, designed and spearheaded the drive to create Adirondack Great Camps. He combined his knowledge of Swiss architecture with native materials and built Sagamore, Uncus, Kill Kare, and Pine Knot before he plunged from owning a million Adirondack acres to becoming a desk clerk in a North Creek Hotel.

Great Camps are worth preserving. They not only tell the story of the wealthy during the heydays of the Adirondacks, but also the story of the hundreds who became the support staff. Many of today's generation of Adirondackers trace their roots to wealthy camp service.

Camp Santanoni in Newcomb is falling in disrepair. We, the people of New York State, own it and are now preserving it. It is over one hundred years old and is in better shape than the Victorian homes built at the same time. The self-supporting veranda links five buildings. It was built for durability, using natural materials and in harmony with the environment, each a good reason for preserving it. It truly reflects the "elegant simplicity" of the Adirondack Great Camps.

XVIII

Adirondack Culture

PAINTERS

Artists were among the first to discover the Adirondacks. They have found the Adirondacks to be inspirational and good subjects for their works since the early 1800's. They were among the first to penetrate the wilderness and among the first to share the beauty and majesty of the forested hillsides and glistening waters with the outside world. The line of artists who have found the Adirondacks is endless to this day. Possibly, it is one of the most painted regions of our nation.

When New York State Geologist-in-Chief Ebenezer Emmons made his exploratory trip up Mt. Marcy, our nation's last frontier, Charles Ingraham was with him. His painting of Indian Pass is included in Emmons' report of 1837.

Arthur Tait can be called *the* Adirondack artist. He spent thirty years in the Adirondacks recording the scenery and life in New York's wilderness. He began his career working in an English art gallery, came to America in 1850, and went to Malone to search for his brother. His love for the Great North Woods began. He returned summer and winter to paint life in the Adirondacks. Eventually he moved to the Loon Lake and Raquette Lake area on a permanent basis.

Tait did 48 of the famous Currier and Ives prints and 44 of his Adirondack paintings for the prints have been found. The Currier and Ives print of Tait's "The Life of a Hunter: A Tight Fix" is considered the rarest of the prints and the less than a dozen in existence are valued at over $10,000 each. The story of the fight with a bear in the painting was given to Tait by a Long Lake guide. Tait had once studied lithography which uses beef suet, goose grease, wax, soap, and stove black in process of making prints from stone plates. He knew it would take his pictures into the American homes.

Adirondack artists such as Tait recorded Adirondack activities that are a source of historical information to this day. The authentic details in paintings provide a picture of how things were done in the Adirondacks. Tapping trees, deadfall traps, equipment, and the garb of the locals and sports are among the many details to be seen in the paintings. We not only enjoy the Adirondack vistas but also the activities pursued by the early Adirondackers.

Winslow Homer was another Adirondack artist of note who painted over 100 Adirondack paintings showing authentic details of life in his day. Homer visited the Adirondacks in the 1870's and made regular visits during the next 38 years. He was a charter member of the North Woods Club near Minerva. Homer also had knowledge of lithography, having been apprenticed at 19 to a Boston lithographic illustrator.

Homer's paintings of the Adirondacks reflect his love of the woods and out-of-door pursuits. Campers, fishermen, hunters, and animals were common subjects of his work. Homer's Adirondack guides have a woodsy know-how that is true to life. His painting of "Two Guides" was the inspiration for the logo of today's outdoor guides' association. Homer did not paint panoramic landscapes; he was interested in showing man's relation to nature.

Jasper Cropsey of the Hudson River School of artists went to the Adirondacks at one time and his giant painting, "The Adirondacks." is a classic. His view of the colorful autumn mountains with boys watering the cows in a mountain stream reflects my own boyhood and that of many who grew up in the Adirondacks.

Over two dozen acclaimed artists include a significant number of Adirondack subjects in their paintings, Names such as Hart, Kensett, Remington, Stewart, Stoddard and Wyant, among others, appear on the list of Adirondack artists. Their paintings not only bring the beauty of the region to the viewer, but also provide another valuable source in the story of our mountains.

MUSIC

Wherever you find man you find his music. Every region of our nation has its music and the Adirondack region is no exception. When the settlers arrived the music came with them. Those who loved the Adirondacks loved to sing about them. Songs of the lives of the hardy inhabitants and the lumber camps have been passed from one next. Today's folk singers carry on a tradition started years ago around the campfires, in the lumber camps, and at the kitchen stoves of the Adirondack pioneers.

Formal music training was not, and is not, a requirement for Adirondack singers. I remember the days when we gathered at the home of one of my uncles and as soon as the meal was finished, out came the instruments. Guitars, banjos, mouth organs, dulcimers, a piano, and, at one time, an accordion were among the available instruments. They were played "by ear." Sometimes it took a minute to recall a tune but once someone hummed a little bit of it, it started and everyone joined in. Sometimes one person knew the words, other times all would sing. The hours spent in just sitting and listening had instilled a lifelong love of country and folk music in me.

William Purves composed "The Adirondac Deer Hunt Galop" in 1853. The well done composition was dedicated to that mighty hunter, John Cheney, with the "kind regards of the composer." It was published by Ceib and Jackson in New York City. John Cheney was one of the first Adirondack guides; he guided near Tahawas in the middle of the 19th century.

C. P. Hallock of Gloversville made his tribute to the Adirondacks in a published song, "Jimmie Creek Song" in 1909. There are two Jimmy Creeks, one on West Hill near Wells and the other on Route 8 near Griffin. His song speaks of Dunham and Finch mountains which leads us to believe that Jimmy Creek is the one near West Hill. His song tells of man's need to get away from the heat in the stifling city to seek respite from the cares of daily strife, concluding, "Oh Jimmie Creek! We come to thee."

A good example of the typical Adirondack musician is Archlus (Pete) Craig of Wells. He passed away several years ago, never having performed for a formal audience, never writing down or publishing his songs, never gaining the notoriety shared by many of today's singers. He simply enjoyed composing songs and sharing them with his friends and neighbors. Pete sang for small groups around the stove in the general store. We have some of his songs today because some were once taped by the general storekeeper.

Pete wrote about his everyday life in the Adirondacks. He wrote songs about the Sacandaga River Valley, about the problems of snow-plowing on the rural roads of the mountains, a song about then-governor Rockefeller and my favorite one, a song about Lee Fountain's Whitehouse tourist business on West Hill. He sang the popular folk sons of the day including the story of the famous Gillette murder trial.

Adirondack folk songs are a great source of history. Pete's song of the Whitehouse tells the complete history of that part of the Adiron-dacks, from its heyday as a tourist attraction to its present "forever wild" use as part of the Forest Preserve. He includes the best description of Adirondack storytelling that I have ever heard:

> "He would tell tales no one could believe,
>> But he grinned as he left us in wonder
>> A'wiping his face with his sleeve."

Peter summarized the history of the Sacandaga River Valley in his song "Sacandaga River."

>> "This old Sacandaga River we all know so well
>> Its whispering waters have a story to tell."

His description of Governor Nelson Rockefeller is unique but one shared by many of his day. The song ends with reference to the amount of tax dollars the Governor spent and how we all love our Governor, but, "we are glad there is only one!"

Too bad Pete and some of the other folk singing song writers of the Adirondacks did not have a publisher or a recording studio. I am certain that our collection of Adirondack music would be richer. However, we are fortunate that today's crop of singers such as Bill Smith, Chris Shaw, Dan Berggren, Peter Gott, and others are searching out those old songs and are recording or sharing them for appreciation by those who love the Adirondacks today.

STEREOGRAPHS—TV OF YESTERYEARS

I recently purchased a stereoscope photograph of Courtney's, number one of a set of 26 cards entitled "Gems of The Adirondacks, Piseco and Lake Pleasant" by William Tucker of Little Falls. Courtney's was a large two-story building in Piseco serving as a hotel. It had two large verandas, up and down, and an adjacent outhouse. It was a family operation. I learned this information from the stereograph, as they are called, one of our earliest sources of Adirondack history.

I also have a stereograph, photo number three in the set, of the Abram's house. Other pictures in the series include Piseco Mountain from Courtney's, the boat landing at Courtney's, and a mirror at Courtney's. It would be a great find to locate these and the other 21 in the set. They leave in the memory "a beautiful little chapter," as Tucker writes, "of the pleasures among the wilds of Piseco and Lake Pleasant."

I have fond memories of the stereoscope. Both of my grandmothers had a stereoscope, patented around the turn of the century, and an associated set of cards or stereographs. Each card, for those who have never peered through the double lenses of a stereoscope, had two like pictures each taken from a slightly different view. In this way, when observed through the double lenses, they two pictures would blend together to form a highly effective 3-D picture.

I traveled around the world and through the Bible, before TV, with stereoscopic pictures. Each card was placed in the sliding focus frame and narrated by my grandmothers. Some were scenes of nature, some of farm buildings and cities, and some were people and animals. Scenes of other countries were popular as well as scenes from the Bible stories. But my favorites were the outdoor scenes and those of the Adirondacks.

Some of the photographs taken by well-known Adirondack photographer Seneca Ray Stoddard appear on stereographs. They are of the best quality and, like all of his photographic work, portray the real Adirondacks. I have one taken at Lake George with a group of fashionable ladies taking a trip in a guideboat protecting themselves from the sun with their parasols. The range of Stoddard's work can be seen in another view I have of Lake George taken from the top of Prospect Mountain.

Another Adirondack series of stereographs called "Gems of the Adirondacks" was done by Baldwin Photos of Keeseville, New York. The cards were oversized and framed in a rustic border. They depict scenes of Ausable Chasm, a popular subject for stereographs. Others included pictures of scenic lakes such as the St. Regis Outlet.

The Ausable Company also produced oversized stereographs of scenes in the chasm. The photos were taken by R. M. McIntosh of Northfield, Vermont. A lengthy description of the Ausable Chasm business was printed on the back of each card, apparently a forerunner of today's TV advertising.

W. Mould and Son, also of Keeseville, did an Adirondack series of 38 stereographs. It includes seven of the old Adirondack hotels, camp scenes, and some lakes and mountains. They, too, are scarce: I have only found one of this set.

Another series which enjoyed popularity was called "American Scenery." Based on the number of cards turning up in the antique stores, it can be assumed that large numbers of this series were printed.

Boats and cabins appear in the photographs along with the usual Adirondack waters and mountains.

"The Picturesque of the Adirondacks" include oversized stereographs by Purviance, photographer and publisher of Philadelphia. The set includes historic photographs such as Paul Smith's Hotel and exceptionally fine scenes of Adirondack lakes.

Steward Wilson, view photographer from Mayfield, New York, advertised "Stereoscopic and large views made to order." He recorded Sacandaga Park on stereographs during its heydays. In later years Wilson became the Sacandaga hermit, taking tintypes of Adirondack visitors.

Several other companies produced outdoor scenes, many taken in the Adirondacks but not identified. The Kilburn Brothers of Littleton, New Hampshire, published a series of outdoorsmen in action. They also did a couple of camp life or a "home in the woods in the Adirondacks" which are worth "a thousand words." The sports, the guides, the game, and the rustic camps come together in a real Adirondack scene out of history.

I have one stereograph with a view of the Lower Saranac Lake in the Adirondacks. It was produced by Hills and Bowers of Burlington, Vermont. The card is a good example of over-commercialization, much as today's TV. The front of the three and half by seven-inch card contains a border of seven commercial ads and the back is entirely covered with another twenty-five, advertising everything from soap to a ten-cent cigar.

It is great to enjoy that old Adirondack stereoscopic pastime on occasion and turn back the pages of time to view some Adirondack history. It is a part of my life and can be an enjoyable part of the lives of those who love the Adirondacks.

EDIBLES

Farmers in the Adirondacks were not always successful in growing a garden. The altitude, with its accompanying short growing season and the rocky soil, worked against them. Yet, there was a food supply available; the forest was filled with produce for those who learned the ways of the wild.

The Native Americans developed a menu of wild food before the first settlers arrived. The original name, "Adirondack," referred to one of the Algonquin tribes. It is believed that when the Mohawks saw the Algonquins eating the inner bark of the white pine trees, they, in derision, called the "Ha-de-ron-dacs" or bark eaters. They had good reason for eating the pine bark; it contained the vitamin C they needed to prevent scurvy.

Onions, widely used today, have a cousin which lives in the Adirondacks. It grows wild and can be found throughout the mountains. The leaves are flat, green, and can be eaten much as we eat scallions. The bulb below the ground can be used in salad, cooking, or in soups. These tasty plants are called leeks. Somewhat stronger than garlic or onions, they should not be eaten before an important date. Sometime the aroma has a delayed reaction. The old Adirondack guide once had a dog who liked to dig and to eat leeks. The guide said that he didn't really mind except "now his bark is worse than his bite!"

Milkweed leaves have been enjoyed for generations. Cooked like spinach, they are a good addition to any meal. Early Adirondackers also learned to eat the "berries" of the milkweed. The small green buds were picked from the top of the milkweed plant before they blossomed out into the reddish flower. These buds were blanched in boiling water for one minute, three times. Cooked for ten minutes, they were served with butter and pepper. Many say they are cheaper and better than broccoli. (Someone should have told President Bush).

Violets cover the ground in the springtime and provide nature's vitamin pill. They are a great source of vitamin C and A, among others. The violet blossoms and leaves can be eaten raw, in salads, in a drink, or mashed up and made into jelly. Violets were a welcomed source of vitamin C in a land where oranges and grapefruit were foreign.

Mushrooms abound in the Adirondacks: some safe to eat, and some not-so-safe. Learning to pick the proper mushrooms is a science and cannot be done overnight. It is better to "apprentice" with an old mushroom picker who is alive and living to pick another day. It is also better to learn one or two easily identified kinds than to take a chance on a wide variety. Many mushrooms have twins; there are some good ones that have a look-alike poisonous one. And the old dime in the water trick does not always work; some poisonous mushrooms do not turn the dime black. Considering the risks, mushrooms are still a delicacy that are worth pursuing in the Adirondacks.

Sumac tea or Indian lemonade is another product of the Adirondack "supermarket." Some like it; some do not. It tastes somewhat like a tangy lemonade. Pick the berries from the common sumac, drop them in water and let them set for awhile, or steep them in boiling water. They are at their best in late summer or early fall.

Indian cucumbers are the hidden delicacies in the list of Adirondack edibles. They are a horizontal, tuber-like root of an Adirondack plant. The plant grows in the damp woods of the mountains and is easily identified by the circle of five to seven leaves around the stem. The blossom and three smaller leaves are at the top of the nearly foot-long stem. The snow white root is pulled out of the ground by digging around the base of the plant with your finger. It can be eaten raw for survival or as a snack, added to a salad or cooked for a vegetable. Plan to leave some when you are digging; taking the roots of all the plants would eliminate future growth.

There are enough Adirondack edibles to prepare a meal that would compete with any restaurant. It can be tasty and full of nutrition. It should be remembered, however, that it is illegal to pick vegetation off the Adirondack Forest Preserve (State land). Legal picking must be done on private land with permission.

MUSEUM IN THE MOUNTAINS

The shortest standard-gauge railroad in the world was found in the heart of the Adirondacks. The total line was five-eighths of a mile. The railroad took its passengers around the Marion River rapids between Raquette and Blue Mountain Lakes. Known as the Marion River Carry Railroad, it had one of the wealthiest board of directors in the world. The board included Chauncey Depew, Collis P. Huntington, J. P. Morgan, Harry Payne Whitney, Alfred G. Vanderbilt, William C. Whitney, and John A. Dix.

The Marion River Carry Railroad was built in 1900 by William W. Durant of the railroad building Durant family. He equipped the line with three old $25 horse-drawn streetcars from Brooklyn and a locomotive from Pittsburgh. They remained in service until 1929 when the railroad was abandoned.

The abandoned Marion River Carry Railroad became the impetus that led to the creation of the Adirondack Museum in Blue Mountain Lake. In 1947, Harold K. Hochschild, Adirondack summer resident and author of *Township 34,* discussed with Blue Mountain House hotel keeper and author of *Adirondack Profiles,* William Wessels, the need to preserve the locomotive and two cars that stood abandoned in the woods near Raquette Lake. The germ of a museum was born.

The Adirondack Historical Association was formed in 1948. William Wessels became president and five years later he sold the Blue Mountain House to the Association for a museum site. Building and collecting began and on August 2, 1957, the Adirondack Museum opened for visitors.

Visitors to the Adirondack Museum always return with expressions of amazement. The range of well-presented exhibits is unexpected in a museum in the mountains. Although seasonal in operation, May to October, the museum staff works year-round in research and preparation of exhibits. Thus it has attained the designation as one of the finest regional museums in our nation.

Pick an Adirondack topic. You will find it in one of the some two dozen buildings at the Adirondack Museum. Guideboats and lake boats, furniture and paintings, logging and mining, wagons and stagecoaches are among the prominent features. Fishing, hunting, hotels, camps, clubs, camping, and winter sports are included in the exhibits. The Adirondack cottages, the school house, a diner, the cupola, the fire tower, and the pavilion add to the visit. The collection of Adirondackana is unsurpassed.

The Adirondack Museum supports a research library. They maintain a book store of books and gifts. They offer a lecture series of Adirondack topics. Adirondack craftspeople can be seen at work on the grounds. School programs and publications help to spread Adirondack knowledge. Special events for guideboat owners, rustic furniture makers, and Adirondack writers are scheduled throughout the season.

The Adirondack Museum is privately owned. It relies on various sources for support such as admission fees, donations, memberships, and grants for operating expenses. The non-profit New York State Chartered museum has continued to grow and expand for over three decades.

It is difficult to select the best exhibit at the Adirondack Museum. Some like the photo-belt with its 160 Adirondack photos. The world's largest collection of guideboats is high on my list along with the Adirondack rustic furniture in the cottage. The locomotive and its car attract the children. The art gallery of Adirondack paintings holds a high priority each year. The wooden stature, cabin and "voice" of Adirondack hermit, Noah Rondeau, is unique. The thousands of display items tell their own story. And, all of this and more, sitting on a picturesque Adirondack hillside, should attract non-Adirondackers and Adirondackers alike.

The museum in the mountains does its job well. It tells the history of the Adirondacks, its people, and their relationship to the majestic Adirondack environment with dignity and thoroughness. The Adirondack Museum is a great place to visit—and I wouldn't mind living there!

VISITOR INTERPRETIVE CENTER

Some have never heard of "VIC." It is no wonder; VIC hides out in the northwest corner of the Adirondacks. It takes up to a three-hour drive from the fringes of the Adirondacks to reach it. VIC is the nomenclature for the Adirondack Visitor Interpretive Center. The Visitor Center at Paul Smiths opened in May of 1989 under the auspices of the Adirondack Park Agency.

The Adirondack Visitor Center is more than a tourist information center. The more than five miles of interpretive trails, with some for wheelchair and stroller access, provide an efficient and effective Adirondack experience. The exhibits and computer "touch screen" information centers are state-of-the art. Information on lodging, camping, trails, and recreation is available in English, French, and Spanish. Special programs are scheduled on a regular basis. Adirondack guides spend time at the center sharing their expertise on the mountainous region. Adirondack story tellers and musicians appear on a regular basis. Slide and film multi-media programs are professionally done. An ongoing lecture series is offered by SUNY College of Environmental Science and Forestry. A book and gift shop is available at the center as well as group tours and school programs.

Everything is free at the VIC, thanks to New York's taxpayers, commercial underwriters, and the Friends of the Adirondacks. The Friends support the Adirondack Park Institute, Inc. which supplies educational programs for students and teachers and a special "Saturdays are for Kids" program.

The VIC building is built of wood and stone, somewhat reminiscent of the Adirondack Great Camp buildings. The trails include bridges, boardwalks, and observation decks. A viewing deck attached to the main building provides a picturesque view of the Adirondacks. A comfortable lounge with Adirondack log furniture contains view-windows to the wilderness. The staff at the VIC is well-qualified and helpful. Volunteers support the center in many capacities. The grounds include a Native American Peace Tree, picnic areas, identified plantings, and a playground.

The VIC is there to visit throughout the year. It is open daily from nine to five with the exception of Christmas and Thanksgiving. During the warm season it stays open until 7:00 p.m. daily. Motorists on Route 30 pass the entrance to the VIC about one mile above Paul Smiths College. The building cannot be seen from the road; it is surrounded by a wooded area.

The Adirondack Teacher Center is also located in the VIC. The Teacher Center, a state-funded facility providing programs for educators, works in cooperation with the VIC. One of the major collaborative programs is a Partnership for an Environmentally Sound Future. School children throughout the region have become part of a computer network comparing their lives and environment with those "outside" and supplying those outside the Park an awareness of the environmental, natural, and cultural resources of the Park. It is a far-reaching and much-needed program if we are to raise a generation who appreciates New York's great wilderness.

A second visitor center was opened in 1990 near Newcomb on Route 28N. It reflects the offerings of the main center including trails, exhibits, and information. Other similar satellite sites may someday be located at each of the entrances to the Adirondack Park. They are needed in the eastern Adirondacks and in the south.

A newsletter, "The Adirondack Observer," is published each season by the VIC. It lists the scheduled programs and includes articles of interest about the six million-acre Adirondack Park. The next time you are in the North Country, plan to make a stop at the Adirondack Park Visitor Interpretive Center.

AUSABLE CHASM

Ausable Chasm, one of nature's awe-inspiring wonders, has been attracting people to the Adirondack region for almost 125 years. This two-mile gorge, cut by the Ausable River waters on their way to Lake Champlain, has attracted visitors from around the world. And it is as exciting today as it was in 1870 when it first became a commercial attraction. Natural beauty is as immortal as the "rock of ages."

Visitors to Ausable Chasm take a tour through walks, stairways, bridges, and boats. The boat ride through the flume is an unforgettable experience. Natural occurrences of rock formations have been appropriately named: Elephant's Head, Pulpit Rock, Jacob's Ladder, The Mecca, The Cathedral, Mystic Gorge, Table Rock, Sentinel, The Devil's Oven, and The Devil's Punch Bowl. The names reflect man's interpretation of the massive stone formations at this geological wonder.

We owe our enjoyment of Ausable Chasm to swift-running water. The Ausable River ground out the geological formation of the chasm. The sedimentary layers were carved and hewn like a sculptor working with clay. The right rock was in the right place at the right time so that today we have a natural wonder to enjoy.

The French word "ausable" means "to the sand" probably referring to the sandy shore of Lake Champlain. The town spells the word AuSable, while the chasm has traditionally put it in one word.

Ausable Chasm was first visited in 1865. William Gilliland, pioneer landowner who planned a baronial estate in the Great North Woods, recorded his visit to Ausable observing, "One would think that this prodigious cleft was occasioned by an earthquake." Gilliland would have been better off developing the chasm; he lost his Adirondack enterprise during the Revolution and in later years died wandering through his former lands in the wilderness. He left his name to Wilsboro and his wife's name to Elizabethtown.

A Philadelphia publication, "The Northern Tourist," devoted a section to Ausable Chasm in 1879. It was illustrated by old woodcuts and described the journey to Ausable: " . . . we came to a wooden shanty, where our party indulged in a glass of a mild beverage known as ginger pop, prior to commencing a most wonderful boat ride."

It is again time for a visit to Ausable Chasm. Load your party into the car, get a bottle of ginger pop, and take a trip to the beauty and the boat ride found in the Adirondack Park's northeast corner, Ausable Chasm.

Today's Ausable Chasm remains because man, the "superfactor" appeared on the scene. The presence of a power dam above Rainbow

Falls keeps the river from accelerating the headward erosion. In their natural state rivers cause rapids and falls further and further upstream as they develop, thus changing the configuration of the river below.

The Ausable Chasm has been advertised widely for many years. Old brochures, postcards, and picture books pop up in the flea markets from time to time, extolling the offerings of this natural attraction. A reprint of an article on the formation of the chasm was taken from a 1942 *Scientific Monthly Magazine* and made into a picture and story book. Souvenir books with their colored pictures vividly illustrate how the buildings and man-made structures have changed or are gone while the natural beauty remains the same.

Those who visit Ausable Chasm have a wide choice. They may simply stand and view the chasm. They may climb or walk the trails. They may take the boat ride down the swift rapids. The beauty is there whatever the choice. We have never been disappointed when we had to pay to enjoy natural occurrences while some of mankind's tourist's traps lead to a let down.

The Adirondack Northway has opened up the opportunity to visit Ausable chasm to greater numbers. Exit 34 on I-87 at Keeseville is about two miles from the chasm on old U.S. Route 9.

Epilogue

SACANDAGA SOLITUDE

Solitude at the Sacandaga Campsite is something to be savoured, that is, put your humanness on hold there among the stately pines and let nature, through your senses, overwhelm your very being. Solitude, sublime!

The moving hush of the clear cold waters of the Sacandaga as they take their journey to the Hudson and the sea can also move through your hearing to those sound bytes in your brain, there to replace the din of daily living in a sometimes dismal world.

The silvery sunlight sparkling off the water and mixing with the patchwork shadows of the trees glistens through your eyes and takes its place in the myriad recesses of the sight center. The manifold greens of the summer trees fill the mind with amazement at nature's inherent artistic talent.

The smells of nature are mixed and blended until no one scent subdues the others. There is a whiff of fish, a pinch of pine, and the faint odor of a campfire. The nose intakes the smells of the woods and triggers stored memories of long ago, lazy days of summer in the Adirondacks.

Nature has feelings and those who take the time can feel the stored-up stress leave the body and soul among the fabrics of nature. Hug a tree; the rough bark of the giant, centuries-old, white pine has a feel of solidarity. Pick up a river-washed rock and rub your hands over the perfected smoothness. A broken rock with its sharp edges has a different story to tell. Climb on a big boulder and bring out the permanence of nature. Feel the breezes while they clear the air and bring new life to the human creature.

Nature sets a fine table for those who want to taste the out-of-doors. Berries and nuts and roots are there for the taking. Greens for every one of man's illnesses grow abundantly in the wilderness. Ginseng for the blood, purslane for the heart, St. John's Wort for depression, boneset for pneumonia, and the list goes on; nature has a way of caring for body and soul.

How long has it been since you took off your shoes and felt the warm earth beneath your feet, or massaged your aching feet among the rocks in a cool mountain stream? When did you lie down in a clearing and listen to the grass grow? Some of life's most precious moments are relegated to our youth and left behind in our journey through adulthood.

How long has it been since you walked through a damp and quiet woodland glade or hiked a hill with a view that belongs in a landscape painting? Why does life keep us from nature's gifts that are there for us and will be there long after we are gone?

Some say that mankind has a seventh sense—one that might possibly lie beyond our understanding—something that the human mind cannot fully comprehend. It combines all of the senses including the intuitive sixth sense, into one. It exists in the realm of an unseen and unknown relationship between man and nature. We are all bonded with Mother Earth and Mother Earth is part of us. In my estimation, it is unnatural for humankind to live a life ignoring the natural world. Severing our ties with the timeless terrain beneath our feet takes its toll on the quality of life itself.

We can be thankful for the foresight of our forefathers—that they preserved a bit of our world for us. Thanks to them we can go to the recesses of the Adirondacks, including the Sacandaga Campsite, the forested mountains, the clear waters, the somber glades and sunlit glens, and think like a child once again, allowing our senses to put that whole world together in the seventh sense of our minds. It is then we truly experience the purest sense of life.

About the Author . . .

Don Williams is an Adirondacker. He was born and raised in the Adirondacks and has never lived or worked more than five miles from the Adirondacks. Growing up at the ingress of the Northville-Lake Placid Trail provided ample opportunity for him to experience the Adirondacks, its people, its history, and folklore.

He authored three books of Adirondack and local history: *The Saga of Nicholas Stoner or A Tale of the Adirondacks*; *Nicholas Stoner and the Sammons Boys, or a Tale of the Mohawk Valley*; and *Oliver H. Whitman, Adirondack Guide and Other Stories*. Williams has written over 250 articles for magazines including *Adirondack Life* and the *Journal of Outdoor Education*. He has served as Adirondack regional editor of *New York Sportsman* for over eighteen years. His "Inside the Blue Line" newspaper column has been published weekly for over ten years. His TV show, also called "Inside the Blue Line," ran for over three years in Gloversville and Glens Falls.

Williams has been in great demand as an Adirondack lecturer and storyteller. He has appeared in schools and at organizations throughout the northeast for over twenty-five years. He has taught "The Adirondacks" at grade schools, high schools, colleges, and elderhostel.

Williams, a retired school administrator and licensed Adirondack guide, lives at 23 E. State Street in Gloversville with his wife, Beverly, in a "replicated Great Camp." They have five married children and eleven grandchildren.